D1803458

Having It All

Sydney P. Jarkow

VANTAGE PRESS
New York

FIRST EDITION

All rights reserved, including the right of
reproduction in whole or in part in any form.

Copyright © 1992 by Sydney P. Jarkow

Published by Vantage Press, Inc.
516 West 34th Street, New York, New York 10001

Manufactured in the United States of America
ISBN: 0-533-10116-6

Library of Congress Catalog Card No.: 91-91394

0 9 8 7 6 5 4 3 2 1

This book is dedicated to the people in my life who have given me the opportunity, by their loyalty and help, to take the time to experience the events depicted in this book.

Particular thanks go to my wife, Edna, and my children, Joan, Kenneth and Jerilynne, who I hope were not too anxious during the times that I was on extended trips and out of the country.

Thanks to my business associates, Harold, Arthur, Jeff, Marvin, and Mike, who carried on and did a great job to make our businesses successful. Of course, there were others that I might have forgotten to mention, and if so, please excuse me.

Special thanks to my long-time secretary and friend, Phyllis, who, a long time ago, urged me to start writing of my experiences. Also to Phil, who in his conservative way has kept me financially sound.

I am deeply indebted to the late Elias Krupp, who gave me my first and lasting experience in philanthropy.

In my introduction to the Anti-Defamation League I was fortunate to be put into the hands of Abe Foxman, who has continued to be my mentor and guiding spirit in my relationship with the League. This has been extended to my close friend, Rabbi Mort Rosenthal, who is Director of the Latin American Division and of the Jarkow Institute.

Finally, special thanks to Karen Davis, who led me through the intricacies of becoming an author.

Contents

Introduction	*vii*
One. Early Days	1
Two. Getting Established	23
Three. Africa—The First Safari	50
Four. Returning to Africa Again and Again	67
Five. Stalking Big Prey	93
Six. Tribal Encounters	111
Seven. From Boy Scout to Nazi Hunter	141
Eight. Big Business	159
Nine. The ADL and the Jarkow Institute	173

Introduction

On June 23, 1990, the morning of my seventy-fifth birthday, I remember thinking that I had reached a happy age of life. All the sweet memories of my children's nursery schools, camps, and colleges, all of the business and financial needs that occupied so much of life were behind me. I've always been an optimist—thinking the best of people and life and generally getting it—so I still look forward to the future and to each particular morning even, but the present time just seemed especially good for me. Love for my wife and affection for my family and friends still runs strong. Envy is weak, largely because of the luck the good Lord has given me. I thought then and still think today, a year later, that I am indeed at the happy age.

But then came a marvelous surprise party my children and wife held for me at the Twenty-One Club in New York City. Grandchildren—and even a great grandchild—relatives, long-time friends, and business associates came. I felt blessed and honored by the love they showered on me and by the lengths they went to in order to share memories of me out loud. There was laughter around the table and a few tears. Some episodes I remembered with embarrassment; some I had even forgotten. But I realized that each person was describing just one small part of me, one side of my personality, one or two types of joint experiences.

Now, in the business I've been engaged in all my life—the children's apparel trade—we've never been interested just in parts. We never made or sold just the sleeve or legging, for instance; we made the whole snowsuit. In fact, we never merchandised just one type of garment, like party dresses—we sold the whole line from buntings to baby bottles to bathing suits.

So listening to all those separate, individual memories made me realize the obvious, that I was the only one who could weave together the whole fabric of my life. My wife, Edna, who knows me better and longer than almost anyone else, probably understands 98 or 99 percent of who I am. But even she doesn't see the whole cloth that I'm made of.

That's just a simple fact of life, I know. But it made me aware of an inner urge to preserve my life's events by writing about them. Part of it may be due to my business background; I'm used to taking stock of things, of making up an inventory. I'm also used to balancing books, so although I certainly don't think of myself as getting ready to close down my account, it's natural for me to want to get my house in order. For all those years, I took stock of the business situation; now, I take stock of myself while I can still remember enough to do it.

But there's another reason also for writing about my life—a desire to reach out to my children, grandchildren, and my children's grandchildren so that they know who Dad, Pappy, or whatever else they call me was really like. It's another type of inheritance I want to bequeath them—not just money, material mementos like wristwatches or photographs, but a picture in my own words showing me.

I'd like to think I write not out of vanity or boastfulness. I don't think of myself as being anything other than just an ordinary guy who's had some extraordinary experiences. I've made more than a few bucks, but I've also travelled widely, hunted big game in Africa, and done some independent Nazi-hunting. For the last seventeen years, I've also been involved with the Anti-Defamation League, and through that I've had the chance to meet and talk with many national and international political leaders. I don't claim to have shaped any policy regarding anti-Semitism or any kind of discrimination, but I do believe my opinions on different issues have been valued.

When the idea originally came to me that I wanted to write about my life experiences, I was not thinking of putting them in a book form for publishing. It was more of a private venture. The effect of reaching back in my memory was very much, I suppose, like going through psychological counseling. Although I have never gone through that procedure, I found that the act of putting down my thoughts in longhand on long, yellow legal pads triggered some kind of domino effect where one remembrance led to another and another.

Sitting there, I also had time to reflect on what some of my actions had meant. That's also, I came to realize, what a life story is. Not just a listing of trips, safaris, business deals, and meetings with people but an attempt to see some meaning to it all. In looking back over what I'd done with my life, I saw that I set certain challenges or mountains for myself to climb—in terms of business, adventure, and just personal goals. I can honestly say that I didn't begin with the idea of climbing those mountains just to get to the top; there would have been no point to that. But I did place myself voluntarily into dangerous situations—to a degree, even by writing this book now—in order to learn and to face my own fears and doubts.

I believe I've been blessed with an exciting, interesting, and full life, and for some reason, even people outside my immediate family have asked me to talk about it. That's why I'm putting this in print. But first, I'd like to clear some things up.

Of all my experiences, primarily I get asked about two things: what it was like hunting big game in Africa and tracking down Nazi war criminals in South America.

People often react to those parts of my life with some ambivalence. It's as if they both admire you for it and are appalled by it—"You *hunted* them down?" and "You hunted *them* down?" is the tone behind their questions.

Guests coming to visit for the first time are sometimes surprised that my wife, Edna, decorated our house with the trophies I brought back from Africa—with the heads of Cape buffalo, greater kudu, and sable antelope, for example—that hang on our walls. After all, she's a woman, supposedly more sensitive to surrounding herself with mementos of killing and bloodshed, but eventually, many of these visitors come to admire the sculptural grace of the horns on the animal heads—a quality that attracted me also.

Other people sometimes feel uncomfortable treading on the skins of giraffes, monkeys, and zebras that lie on our floors. One business associate used to tiptoe gingerly over them as if she was afraid of stepping on them too pointedly with the high heel of her shoe. Yet on more than one occasion, I'd also see her slip off her shoe to feel the texture of the hairy hide on her stockinged foot.

Even my Anti-Defamation League friends seem to treat me with ambivalence at times. They especially take a step back from me when it comes to my more active Nazi-hunting days. Executive Director Abe Foxman jokes that the ADL sometimes has to disassociate itself from statements made by lay leaders because the facts aren't true, but in my case the ADL distances itself because the facts *are* true.

I've come to believe that this dual reaction—"You did that?" and "How could you do that?"—may be shaped not only by what I've actually done but by who I am and what I look like. My appearance is not of a rough, tough guy, but of a family man whose tastes run more toward the good things in life, such as our fine home and luxury automobiles. And even in my younger days, except when I was out in the bush, the only facial hair I wore was a neatly clipped, short mustache.

Nor do I look the "spy" type with my trenchcoat collar pulled up, darting suspicious glances out from under the rim of my fedora, although I wore hats to business from the 1930s to the 1960s.

I don't think I'm vain, but I know what people see when they look at me—a fairly well-dressed man with a full head of white hair, attractive in a Douglas Fairbanks, Jr., way, I've been told. (When I was younger, with black hair, and he was well known, the comparison was to Don Ameche.) I look, in fact, like the kind of man you'd want for an in-law, for a board member on your favorite philanthropy, or, on one of my good days, for part of your golf foursome. A nice, normal-looking man, in other words. So what was I doing on foot, following the spoor of a lion through the Kalahari Desert or flying over the treetops of the Brazilian jungle with a paid mercenary?

I'm not about to apologize for what I've done, but I do want people, especially those who view the period of the 1950s–1970s as remote historical decades, to understand *why* I acted the way I did. To do that, you have to know or remember what the flavor of those years was like.

When I started seriously thinking about Africa in 1956, most of the Western world was still experiencing a period of postwar expansiveness and prosperity. In America, under President Eisenhower, the gross national product rose to $408 billion and the Dow Jones average reached the milestone mark of 500.24 points. We drove high-styled, long-finned, low-roofed cars and didn't worry about the cost, economically or environmentally, of putting gas in the tank.

In fact, the word *ecology* was barely in the dictionary, much less on people's lips. Africa still seemed a land of unlimited territory and resources, which, quite frankly, were still there for the white man to take and enjoy. On late afternoons, the wooden veranda of Nairobi's Norfolk Hotel and the Delamere Bar became the mingling place of elegantly tailored men and women—hunters and owners of vast coffee plantations, wearing neatly pressed khaki bush jackets or crisp, white linen suits, with their wives in soft, flowing, flowered dresses.

They'd meet to gossip and chat over their "fives' " or cocktails—pink gins and dry martinis usually—served by silent black Africans with impassive faces. Although the voice of African nationalism was beginning to be whispered by native tribespeople, it wouldn't be heard by the colonial whites until later. I'd meet Jomo Kenyatta and Tom Mboya in a detention camp for rebel Kikuyu tribesmen and Mau Mau terrorists in 1958, but it wasn't until 1963 that Kenyatta became the legitimate president of an independent Kenya, with Mboya as one of his main advisers.

When I started going to Africa, the majority of countries with names like the Bechuanaland, the Congo, Rhodesia, and Tanganyika were still colonial territories of Britain, France, and Belgium. In 1960 alone, seventeen of them became independent nations. Not only did their names change to Botswana, Zaire, Zimbabwe, and Tanzania, for example, but attitudes toward the white *bwana* or *baas* did also, even though the impact wouldn't reach back into the bush and the savannahs until much later.

When I first went on safari, the Mount Kenya Safari Club was being organized by Hollywood movie star William Holden with funds from a rumored Cleveland gambler. But no one thought the worse of them and other entertainment celebrities, political statesmen, and business magnates like Walt Disney, Prince Bernhard of the Netherlands, and Lord Delamere, who became charter members of it. In fact, it became almost an honor to be asked to join the exclusive ranks of big-game hunters—so much so that after Kenya became independent, political leaders Jomo Kenyatta and Tom Mboya, whose Kikuku clansmen still hunted game as a way of life, also joined the club. Interestingly, it was many of these hunters, along with African professional hunters, who would ultimately play an active role in trying to save African wildlife in the 1970s and 1980s.

As for me, I can say I never killed wantonly. I shot for the pot to feed myself and the trackers and native gun bearers who accompanied me. I aimed for the perfect trophy and having gotten the specimen I wanted, I then went on. I've shot many trophies and been cited in the *Rowland Ward Gamebook*, which is like the *Guinness Book of World Records*, six times and never more than once for any animal species. I've even turned down the chance to hunt elephant and tigers in India when I felt the odds were too great against the animal to regard it as sport.

I went to Africa initially for the adventure and excitement. I kept returning to it out of love. Something about being there satisfied or completed a part of my life that was missing here, a part that had nothing to do with my wife or family. If Africa is the birthplace of mankind, as many experts believe, it certainly gave birth to a different side of Sydney Jarkow. To find out completely who I am, you have to see what I saw and did in Africa. So that's why so much of this book is about Africa—because it's an important part of me, as much as growing up in Brooklyn is, marrying my childhood sweetheart, or working for the ADL now.

I know that materially I could be considered a successful man. At least, my children and the IRS think so! But somewhere I once read that a man is a success who has lived well, laughed fine, and loved much. That a man can be deemed a success if he's gained the respect of intelligent men and the love of children; if he's filled his space, accomplished his task, and left this world a better place than he found it, whether it's by rescuing a poor soul, writing the perfect song, or looking for the best in others and giving the best he had.

By these measures, I hope I'll be judged a success. By this book, I hope I've given some measure of the substance of my life.

Having It All

Chapter One

Early Days

Born in 1915, during the first year of World War I, I was given the Hebrew name Shalom by my parents. In English, I was called Sydney Peace Jarkow. Although I like to think I've helped bring peace to some people by helping them work out problems or reconcile their differences, there's been another side to me too—not the peacemaker or "fireman" who put out fires or problems at work, as I once told my young children, but the adventurer who depended on alertness and an ability to stalk prey and instinctively go for the kill, whether it was on the Serengeti plains of Africa, in the apparel showrooms of Manhattan's garment district, or in the South American hideaways of Nazi war criminals.

I was the youngest of five boys, with a younger sister, Adele, born eleven years after me when my mother was about forty-six years old. My parents apparently believed in spacing out their children because there were twenty years separating my oldest brother from myself. He must have been one hell of a guy because as a young man, he served as a fill-in or double for Rudolph Valentino, the star of silent movies. Because of the wide difference in our ages, we were not very close growing up; in fact, my three elder brothers were rarely home when I was young. But we all tolerated each other, and there was a comfortable relationship between us.

I don't really remember much about my childhood before age twelve. I do know that I grew up in a fine section of Brooklyn called Crown Heights, which was full of stately, Victorian-style homes. I don't remember much about our house except it must have been large because it eventually became a small, private hospital long after we sold it and moved out. We also had another summer home, a half hour away, in Seagate, a private community on the shore of New York Bay with its own private police department at the time. It was separated from the Brooklyn streets around it by an iron gate.

Both my parents were Russian Jews; in Russian you use a K instead of the letter J and a V instead of a W, so we once figured out that if you make those substitutions, the name Jarkow looks a lot like the name of the Russian city Karkov. Probably when my grandparents came here, there was some confusion over language in going through the U.S. Immigration Department and the American official may have put down the name of their hometown for their family name.

By the time I was born, both my parents were completely assimilated into American ways; I grew up without any religious education and never had a bar mitzvah or heard a word of Yiddish—two things I've come to regret as I've gotten involved with Anti-Defamation League work.

I've been told that my father had important connections through his business and that often judges and other bigwig politicians would visit our home. He had come over here as a young man and worked as a steam-fitter in the plumbing trade. Somehow or other he got involved with manufacturing parts for the pleating and stitching machines used in the women's wear industry, and that's where he made his money. My mother had help in the house while my father had a black man, Hilton, who lived with us and worked as a valet, chauffeur, and chief handyman. (Neither my father, I'm told, nor I were ever good at fixing things with our hands. Even today, it's my wife, Edna, who makes small repairs in our house, not me.)

Already, you can see, my story is not a traditional rags-to-riches Horatio Alger tale of a boy from an immigrant family, rising above poverty and his ethnic background, in his climb to become successful. We always lived in nice neighborhoods and we always had our own house, not a cold-water apartment in a tenement building.

I remember my father, Jacob, being a big, burly, good-looking man, who was very affectionate. One of my few memories of him involves an incident when I was around eight years old and had come home late. My father was angry enough to punish me, and in my desire to avoid punishment, he chased me around and around our mahogany dining-room table. After circling around quite a few times, he finally caught me and as he reached me he broke out laughing, so I got away lucky.

But he had another side to him also because another vivid memory of him is of a fistfight he got into right in front of our Seagate home when I was about five or six years old. It was on a quiet Sunday morning, and our expensive Pierce Arrow car had gotten stuck. My father, one of my older brothers, and Hilton, his black valet, were pushing it to get it started when suddenly the motor started to turn over, backfired, and made a large noise like bullet shots. Apparently, it must have woken up our neighbor because he came charging out of his house, calling my father a "Jew bastard." My father just started to work on this guy and beat him unmercifully until he was finally pulled off. But that's the only time I remember him losing his temper.

At this time, my father was making his money by being a successful manufacturer and importer of ladies' garments. But he got involved with an import deal that went completely bad. He lost his business in about 1925-1926, a few years before the Great Depression of the 1930s. For a while, the only money coming into the house came from Hilton, who hired out to work for other people and contributed a part of his wages while he still lived with us. Somehow, my father was never able to cope with this financial bad luck, nor was he ever able to make a success of any business again. Instead, he turned to whiskey for comfort. My mother tried to cover up for him, and he himself was always good to us and never abusive or loud. We still had a great deal of affection between us, and maybe that's better than the luxuries I am sure he would have liked to have given us.

But that period when I was around ten years old is probably one of my most important childhood memories. Our family used to have money, at least to the extent of being quite comfortable, and then we began to have money problems. I was determined that that was not going to happen to me.

By the time I was about twelve or thirteen years old, we had moved to Flatbush, another part of Brooklyn near Ocean Parkway. It was a wide avenue that ran right into Coney Island, a busy beach resort, not far from where we lived. Seeing an opportunity to make some money, I began selling children's trinkets, such as balloons and candy, to pedestrians and people in automobiles who were on their way to Coney Island. I was a skinny boy—despite a diet that included lots of potatoes every day because they were cheap and filling—so maybe that helped.

But I did well and after a short time of working alone, I organized some friends to do the direct selling while I did the distributing from the garage of my home. I was pretty popular because despite my slimness, I was a good athlete. Eventually, some older boys started to inch into our territory, and I found it necessary to protect our distributors by setting up a small team of strong young guys to see that we weren't physically thrown off our territory. That was the first and only time, by the way, I've ever had to use "muscle" to deal with problems at work.

Other boys in the neighborhood saw that they could make some money with us, so they filled our sales team and before long, I was making about a hundred dollars a day on the weekends. At that time, during the 1930s, that was quite a lot of money, but most of it was turned over to my parents.

Giving money to help out the family was never something I was told to do, just something I took upon myself. Despite our financial hardships, I always felt I had loving, caring parents and good family relations, so it seemed very natural to me. Because my older brothers had moved out and started families of their own, they could contribute very little. It was the first of a series of financial obligations I assumed out of a sense of responsibility, but I don't honestly know how I grew up to be that way. I just did.

I do believe, however, that as time went on, I became my father's favorite son. That may have been because I was the youngest male child, but also because I was luckier than my other brothers in business. I always felt badly that he didn't live to be able to enjoy the things I would have been able to give him in his later years.

During my childhood, I never remember my mother, Tina, being anything but sweet or well-dispositioned. If she was disappointed in the change of our family fortunes, worried about paying bills, or angry with my father, she never let anything show. In fact, I always remember her singing around the house as she went about her chores—a habit I seem to have inherited.

Standing next to my father, she was small and delicately built. She never seemed to assert herself very much except for one episode that occurred years later, after my father had died in 1947, and she was living in a comfortable retirement hotel facility. It was near my home in Rockville Centre, Long Island, so my family and I could visit her often.

I usually made it a practice on my Tuesday-night visits to bring about forty to fifty Mello Roll's ice-cream desserts to all the guests at the hotel. Although their average age was about seventy-five, they'd all gather eagerly around me like children when I handed out the treats. But I noticed after the fourth or fifth time I did this that my mother seemed to be angry, instead of proud. When I asked her why, her response was indignant. "I am your mother and I expect more consideration from you," she said.

From then on, whenever I came I brought her a pint of ice cream while everyone else just got a regular Mello Roll bar. That showed her as being more important than the other old folks, and it was the only time I remember her ever demanding something from me.

But back to my youth. Because of my good track record in high school, I received an athletic scholarship to Penn State University. I went there intending to study medicine. I'd wanted to be a doctor for as long as I could remember. As a boy, I'd literally run after ambulances and there'd be times when I found ways to sneak into hospital emergency rooms. My scholarship covered tuition, books, room and board, and my father sent me about $2–3 every other week for spending money. Remember this was around 1933–1934, during the middle of the Depression!

Halfway through my sophomore year, I learned that my father was doing without lunches in order to send me that small amount of pocket money, and I just could not accept that situation, so I quit school. I took a bus from State College Town to Brooklyn, and the family was devastated because of my decision. I would have been the first in the family to get a college education.

So there I was, on the edge of my twenty-first birthday, and I knew I had to get a job immediately. The day after my return to Brooklyn, I left my home about 7:30 A.M. to ride the subway into Manhattan. I had no idea whom I'd see or where I'd go. I didn't even think about the kind of job I wanted. On the train, I met a neighbor who asked me what I was doing. When I told him I was looking for work, he suggested that I come to his office, where he offered me a job at eight dollars a week as a combination porter and packer. He was a jobber or wholesaler in general dry goods who was slowly beginning to specialize in children's clothing.

I quickly accepted his offer and worked for the A. S. Lazarus Company for about seven years from 1936–1943. The company seemed to need me, and I grew fast in it, moving from position to position. I began by sweeping the floors and packing merchandise in the back room, but I went on to become the head salesman, the general manager, and the chief of all purchases.

Lazarus was a hard-driving, difficult man to work for. He ran the company like a despot, and we were at constant odds with one another. But I give him credit for instilling in me a strong appreciation of the work discipline for business associates, employees, and myself. It also gave me a chance to establish myself in the infants' and children's wear industry in its earliest years. Up until a few years before this time, infants' wear was considered part of the dry-goods industry and not something separate on its own.

A lot of people think of the garment industry as being full of flashy, loud, *What Makes Sammy Run?*-type men and women. Fast-talking salesmen wearing shiny, gold pinky rings and snappy sharkskin suits; gum-chewing, bored receptionists; out-of-town buyers expecting to be entertained day and night; and lecherous men pinching models' bottoms. I can't speak for the garment industry as a whole, but the children's wear industry definitely was *not* that way.

We were a smaller group of people, mostly small firms, and a lot of business was done initially with just a handshake. Unlike the ladies' wear business, most of our suppliers, manufacturers, jobbers, and skilled and unskilled factory workers weren't Jewish. Most of the buyers were women, who always showed up at showrooms wearing hats and gloves, and maybe that fact, plus the nature of our product, accounted for the quieter tone of our business.

At any rate, I worked my way up to the top of the A. S. Lazarus Company and along the way learned about almost every aspect of the business. The one part I never really liked was the numbers part. When I went into business on my own, I made sure to pick a good accountant to work with and later on my son, Ken, took over a part of the various responsibilities.

But those days were still a long time off. First, I proposed to my high school sweetheart, Edna, and married her in 1938. We had met at a high school football game when she was striking-looking fifteen-and-one-half-year-old redhead with green eyes and I was seventeen years old. For a while I went to Abraham Lincoln High School, but then I transferred to James Madison High School. We hung out with the same group of neighborhood kids, and I remember Edna watching me play ball a lot. She claims she chased me until she caught me, and I let her think so.

When I went away to Penn State, we wrote to each other. At school, most of my time was spent in studying or in running track for my scholarship, so I was too busy to date and not really interested in it anyway. Somehow, Edna and I had just become a couple and when I came home to Brooklyn, we picked up where we left off.

During those Depression days, our dates might be an occasional movie and a trip to Rhoda's Beach, a sort of lover's lane. But let me assure our children and grandchildren who may be reading this that although the chemistry was more than just right, this was before the age of sexual permissiveness, so my wife's virtue was intact when we married! One of the things Edna claims that set me apart from the other neighborhood boys was that I treated her with what she calls "decorum"—in other words, that I never took advantage of her and stopped when she said "stop," although, God knows, I certainly didn't want to!

Edna's parents weren't too happy with her decision to marry me. They thought I was a skinny kid who didn't make a hell of a lot of money and they wanted Edna to marry a doctor. But Edna says she saw something in me—ambition, responsibility, and feeling for my family. One day when we were talking about our dreams, she told me hers was to own a Rolls Royce, and maybe she sensed that I'd be able to get it for her. I did nearly forty years later!

As for me, I wasn't able to put it in words at the time, but I saw in Edna someone who'd love and adore me. Edna admits that I came first in her life, then came our children. As an example, she and the children would always wait for me to come home, even if it was as late as 7:30 P.M., before eating dinner. She told me once she had never had a strong father image, so she felt it was important for her to give our children one of me. So I got a great deal of emotional security from her love. It's partly because of her support and confidence in me that I was bold enough to strike out on my own in business and even to go off to Africa.

That belief in me was really needed when we finally got married nearly five years after we had met. I was earning a little more than $35–40 a week. Edna worked also as an orders clerk for a baking company—between us we brought home about $75 a week and our rent was about $45–50 a month. I still remember the name of our apartment building—the Casa del Ritz on Nineteenth Street between Avenues L and M in Brooklyn. Things were tight but we were young and full of hope.

Our first daughter, Joan, was born in 1940 and a year later, after Pearl Harbor Day, December 7, 1941, the United States officially entered World War II. I kept on working for A. S. Lazarus and expected to be drafted anytime. By the time I was called down to the army induction center, it was 1943 and my son had just been born. It was on a day when they must have been processing close to ten thousand men and all I remember about the physical exam was wearing shoes and a hat and nothing in between.

In the late afternoon, they began picking out men who would go directly to officers' candidate school without going through basic training first. I was proud when they chose me to be one of the handful of men they selected. We were immediately inducted into the army and told we had forty-eight hours to wrap up our personal and business affairs before being shipped out.

I was sent to a military camp somewhere in Alabama, I believe. We were going through training under heavy artillery firing and on the second or third day I happened to be standing near a very heavy artillery burst and went deaf. The army doctors who examined me found that I had punctured both of my eardrums; also, apparently I had had a mastoid when I was a baby, which had gone undetected by the examining doctors and that loud burst damaged my hearing permanently.

They sent me back to a New York hospital, and gradually my hearing started coming back. But it never got better than 75–80 percent of what it had been, so the army offered me a choice of taking a desk job in the service or of signing a waiver of no responsibility on the government's part. I didn't want to spend my army time in an office, so I signed the paper and that released me from the army.

It put me in a very uncomfortable situation. All my friends and peers were going off, and some of them were fathers also. My closest childhood friend, Kelly, had gone, and it just seemed strange for one of us to be doing something without the other doing it too. Forget about wanting to go as a Jew or as a young man; I just wanted the chance to show my stuff as a proud American, so the whole period was very disappointing to me. I tried to do what I could by becoming the leader of a local auxiliary group, and we got very involved in night work and maintaining blackouts, but it wasn't the same thing as actually being in the service and I've always regretted it.

Maybe because I had been medically disqualified to fight in the war or maybe because I knew Lazarus's son, Ed, would ultimately take over the business, I became a little itchy and wanted to strike out on my own in business. Apparently, my reputation in the infants' wear field was quite good because when people found out I was available and wanted to be in my own business, a lot of them approached me about joining forces with them.

But I wanted to start something of my own. My wife and I had about four hundred dollars in savings; our second child, Ken, had just been born; and I had an insurance premium to pay, which left us with exactly nothing.

The man I finally chose as a partner was an accountant who represented two brothers in the toy business. He put up forty-six hundred dollars, and I put up the four hundred dollars after getting an extension on the life-insurance policy premium. Best of all, my partner agreed to let me operate the business without any interference. So in 1943, I became a parent twice over: once to my son, Ken, and once to my company, Sydney Infants Wear, Inc., in October 1943. Our company was a wholesaler or jobber of infants' and children's wear.

I still remember my father coming in to see me shortly after we had opened up. Although he was quite ill at the time, he proudly inspected the office and stockroom and then he sat down for a talk. Almost apologetically, he told me he was sorry he was unable to be of any help to me, but he still had some advice for me. "Son," he said, "there are two ways to be successful in business. You have to be either a genius or you have to work hard, and let me tell you the Jarkows are *not* geniuses."

I took that advice to heart. There were times when I worked so late that I fell asleep on the shipping tables only to wake up at 6:00 A.M. and start my day all over again. As a matter of fact, the office was right near the Hotel McAlpin, which had a pool and gymnasium, and I took out a membership there so I'd have a place to bathe and change my clothes. People who knew me during my early business career have often said I was very hard-working, but I never felt that I was, probably because I loved what I was doing.

Not many businesses were starting up at this time, especially in the infants' and children's wear industry. Within the next four or five years, as the war wound down, there would be 114 companies in the wholesale infants' business, but by the end of the 1940s, only three of us would be left.

For the time being, though, I had an advantage.

My accountant partner represented the Gund Company, manufacturers of stuffed animals, and part of our agreement was that I'd distribute their product in my wholesale company. So I was getting merchandise from them at a time when a lot of companies didn't have any merchandise to sell. I also had built up a good rapport with many of the mills, so I got merchandise from them like infants' blankets, sheets, and pillow cases, which were still in short supply.

Since they were still on a war-time quota basis, they did it out of the goodness of their hearts. There was only one man I met during that time, from a plant in Allentown, Pennsylvania, who asked for a bribe, but I turned him down and eventually he went out of business.

But the war and my not being in the army acted to my disadvantage about three or four months after I went into business on my own. We were the wholesalers of the baby pillows that mothers put in cribs and carriages. Each pillow had to have a U.S. Department of Labor tag showing what the contents were and a sticker indicating that a one-cent tax had been paid. Apparently the pillow manufacturer had shipped an order and forgotten to sew the tags on. An inspector from the Department of Labor picked up about ten of our pillows at the Abraham and Strauss Department Store in downtown Brooklyn, and I got a summons and was subpoenaed to appear at court.

The whole thing involved ten pillows or ten cents, so my partner suggested I answer the summons myself without hiring a lawyer. I went downtown to the courthouse and found that this was a criminal procedure, so I waited for my tiny, little case to come up. I was surrounded by huge cartons of nylon hose and other boxes of confiscated merchandise that had been seized on the black market or because they had violated the Office of Price Administration's regulations, which had been put into effect to make sure companies weren't taking advantage of wartime material shortages.

All these cases came up before mine, and the judge, an older man with a long Polish name, handed down very severe sentences in each instance. When I finally approached the bench, he took one look at me, saw a young man, and started a tirade about avoiding the draft and working in the black market.

I couldn't figure out what he was ranting about, so I interrupted and said, "I think you're making a mistake here, Your Honor. Do you know what's involved here?" He shut me up and kept up his tirade until finally I shouted back, "Your Honor, there's just ten cents involved here and it's the mistake of the pillow manufacturer." Well, he got so mad at me that he had the court clerk call the attendants in and they put me in prison. I had to call my partner to bail me out and pay the fine just because the judge thought I was a draft-dodger!

This was one of the rare times I actually called on my partner for help. Although he was an accountant, I only saw him for financial statements, which then were done about every six months. I did, however, send him his weekly paychecks. Luckily, we did very well— so well that in 1945, I took my first business trip outside the continental United States. Looking back now, what's interesting about the trip is that it shows how I was eager to jump into adventure despite being a young man with a young family and business to think about.

About 1945, my business was starting to expand

and I got involved in the purchase of a factory in Mayaguez, Puerto Rico, which manufactured girls' and ladies' "skorts"—a combination of shorts and a skirt. My accountant partner from Sydney Infants Wear had nothing to do with this deal. One of my two partners in this independent venture was the inventor of the skort; the other was in charge of production, while my responsibility was administration and marketing. We purchased the factory in Mayaguez at a relatively low price, and that also included a 45-foot boat, which we decided to give out to charter.

Shortly after our purchase, we had two buyers from a major, national department chain come to tour the plant, so we decided to entertain them on the boat. Our destination was an island about fifty miles offshore of Mayaguez; we had heard it had been used by Germans as a source of guano. Guano, or bat droppings, had commercial value as fertilizer and was widely available on the island, since it was almost totally cavernous and filled with bats.

We loaded up with supplies for five or six days and left on a Friday night—we three owners, the two buyers, and two Puerto Rican seamen we hired from the charter company. But on the first day out, we ran into problems. The weather was changing, and we cut our speed so we'd approach the island by sunrise. As evening progressed into night, the weather got more violent. Since we were in sight of the island, we decided to circle it and cruise as close as we could. The winds got stronger and we became more concerned for our safety because the boat seemed to be drawn to the cliff-side of the island, which rose like a mountain from the sea. The other side of the island showed flatter terrain—a few sandy beaches and some small houses.

To add to our problem, we also found out that the electrical system on the boat was failing, which meant no contact with our home base.

After talking it over, we decided to run the boat onto a sandy beach on the island, tie it up, and move onto shore. Within thirty yards of the beach area, we found the waterline just about touched the bottom of the hull. Since the winds were drawing us toward the island, we decided to beach the boat by tying it up to a tree. But the two Puerto Rican seaman refused to go overboard with a line and tie us up—neither of them could swim, they said. The other men weren't in good condition, so I tied the line around my stomach, jumped in, and swam to shore.

What we didn't see as we approached the beach in the boat became very apparent to me in the water—a huge number of water rats! But I finally managed to tie up the boat, and we drew it up on the shore even though it was listing to one side.

By the time we landed, the sun had started to come up sharply. One of my partners and I decided we'd take the two shotguns we'd brought along on the boat and explore the island. We headed off toward the area where people must have lived, although judging by the housing, there couldn't have been more than twelve to fifteen people on the island. We tried to reach the houses through the open-ended caves or tunnels that honeycombed the island, but the bat droppings were so thick and slimy inside them that it was almost impossible to walk.

We did see lots of odd-looking animals. As we later learned, it seems that some Germans, who had left by submarine two or three years earlier, had originally brought domesticated animals with them. But these animals had since reverted to the wild, so we saw cats larger than dogs, pigs with long, skinny spitting snouts, and lots of large rats.

We got back to the boat and decided we'd try to find a path to the house by means other than through the caves and tunnels. The brush was heavy, but we found a pathway. The house was in fairly good condition, so we knew we could use it in an emergency, but since one of the men with us had a heart condition, we continued to stay with him near the boat. We soon discovered that there was no way to get the boat back into the water and with no ship-to-shore radio facilities, we were veritably shipwrecked.

Since we had taken provisions for five or six days, we knew that no one from the plant or the marina would worry about us. We were now on our second day of being on the island, so we decided to try to signal a passing boat or an airplane. By the fourth day, we were getting really concerned when a navy plane stationed at Fort Raimey Air Force Base spotted us about midday and the pilot circled to indicate he saw the white sheets we were waving. About ninety minutes later, two helicopters flew over the island and lowered a chair. We sent the ill man back to Mayaguez, and with the help of two sailors from the helicopter who stayed behind with us, we got the boat back in the water.

We returned to port in relatively good shape, and the first thing I did was to reprimand the manager of the marina for sending us out with two men who knew very little about seamanship and who couldn't even swim! He looked at me quizzically and after speaking to the two men came back to me laughing like hell. When I asked him why he was laughing, he stopped to tell me that these two guys could probably swim around the island of Puerto Rico if they had to. But they knew that at night and in the early morning, the sharks came close to shore for feeding. They must have said to each other in Spanish, "Let one of these jerks go."

I may have been a jerk for jumping into the water, but since I was by far the youngest one on board, I felt that I had to do my part.

By 1948, there was some economic softening in the infants' and children's industry. It was happening in other industries as well, and my first and only partner in Sydney Infants Wear indicated that he wanted to get out. Dissolving our partnership was fine with me, but I wondered how we could do it without hurting the financial structure of our company. My partner proposed that I buy out his share, which amounted to $105,000. That didn't include another $55,000 in inventory, which he offered to me as a plum if a cash buy-out could occur by a specific date.

During the five years of our partnership, he had drawn a $15,000-a-year salary for his original $4,600 investment, although he had done nothing for the company except the biyearly accounting service. It was basically the same salary I drew, and now I had to find a way to pay him out $105,000 in order to take advantage of the inventory offered to us at no cost. I was able to put together $20,000 from personal savings, but I didn't want to touch company funds because I felt that might weaken the financial structure of the business.

But we still had to find a way to obtain the balance of $85,000. In a moment of desperation, my wife, Edna, suggested I contact Elias Krupp in El Paso, Texas. Elias Krupp was also a distributor of infants' and children's wear and ran a business similar to mine. I had met him during business trips on the road, and since our territory never overlapped, we became friends. He was an older man with no family in his business, and over the years he developed a fondness for me and my family. In fact, he kept trying to "court" me into giving up my business and coming into his as a partner. But my family was growing up and our roots were in New York. Besides, I had always wanted to run my own "peanut stand."

Elias was very well off financially. According to stories he told, he had made his money by following the army of the Mexican bandit and revolutionary Pancho Villa with a well-stocked, horse-drawn wagon. After Villa would plunder a village, he would then barter with my friend for clothing, tobacco, whisky, and all kinds of sundries. My friend obviously knew more about merchandise than Pancho Villa, and so he became a rich man.

It was getting close to my partner's deadline, and we were getting pretty anxious for a solution. I didn't know anyone else with enough financial resources to turn to, so on a Sunday morning, at the suggestion of Edna, I called Elias in Texas and told him I needed $85,000. At that time, asking for that amount would be like asking someone for $5 million today. But without hesitating or even asking what the money was for, Elias said he would send me a check.

But that wasn't the end of my problems. I needed to have the certified check by Monday, the next day, in order to obtain the advantage of not having to include the $55,000 worth of inventory in the payout. When I explained the problem to him, he told me to wait for him to do some local phone-calling and then he'd phone me in New York in about thirty minutes. I don't know how I passed the time, but I did. He phoned back promptly with the name of a major Texas airline pilot who was to arrive late that night at Idlewild Airport in New York, now known as John F. Kennedy Airport, and he'd have the certified check with him. When I asked him how he got a check certified on a Sunday, he said it was easy if you were a bank director the way he was.

To show you what kind of special person Elias was, when I called him back to thank him and to ask how and under what terms he wanted the debt repaid, he kept putting me off and said he'd get together with me. Finally, after a few months, during which time I didn't give him a penny, he came to New York and we decided I'd open a bank account in his name and deposit about four hundred dollars a month into it. We wanted to do it informally at first, but our attorneys advised us against it. "I am sorry about this legal stuff and bookkeeping stuff, but I suppose it is necessary in spite of the fact that we are good friends," Elias once wrote me.

After four years, by 1952, I had accumulated the $85,000 and called to tell him that I had the money, but what did he want to do about the interest on it? He answered that he didn't want any interest, but this just wasn't acceptable to me. Since he had become a chairman of the National Council of Christians and Jews, I made a contribution of what the going interest rate was for the total amount at that time.

It was my first contribution of any sizable amount to a charity, and it was a delicious feeling. Elias Krupp remained my close friend and mentor until his death. He taught me that charity is an obligation that we have to those less fortunate than ourselves and if it cannot be given in money, it should be given in time and services. He also kept me fairly humble about philanthropy by teaching that it's one thing to give time or money without inconveniencing yourself—almost anyone can do that. But when the person giving to charity has to adjust his or her life-style because of it, then that's the true test of a benevolent person.

Chapter Two
Getting Established

Somehow my son, Ken, and my business have always been linked together. He spent some of his high school and college summers working for us in our warehouses; he formally came to work with us in 1965 and when I sold most of my interests in the business in 1985, he did too. But even before that, Ken's life and my business had some significant, mysterious interconnection. Both were born in 1943, as I've stated. And in 1948, both had to ride out a period of turmoil. Economically, the country was going through a mild recession, and I had just bought out a business partner, was trying to pay off a big debt, and run the company completely on my own. As for Ken, he got polio and we almost lost him.

It happened over the summer of 1948 on a vacation weekend for Edna and me. We were playing on a golf course at Saginaw Lake in the Adirondack Mountains of upper New York State when we got word that our housekeeper was trying to reach us with the news that our son had just been taken to the hospital back home on Long Island. We had just twenty minutes to catch a small, commuter airplane back home, and we were in such a hurry that we boarded the plane still wearing our spiked golf shoes. Friends picked us up at La Guardia Airport and told us that Ken had polio and was in the contagious-disease ward at Meadowbrook Hospital, the Nassau County facility.

In the days before Jonas Salk invented the polio vaccine in 1953, it seemed like every summer there was some outbreak of the polio virus among thousands of young children. Infantile paralysis, they called it in those days. Living out in fresh, green suburbia, we never thought much about the crippling disease, but fortunately our housekeeper, Virginia, must have known something about the symptoms—that Ken seemed to have something more than just a common cold or fever—and got him to a doctor in time. We owe our son's life to her quick thinking and actions.

More fortunately, in Ken's case, his breathing wasn't affected, so he didn't need to be placed into an iron lung. But the muscles that affected his arms and legs were attacked, so we got physical therapists to massage them and gently move them to prevent them from painfully tightening up or becoming deformed. As soon as he could, Ken also began an intensive exercise program to help strengthen and retrain his muscles. Our five-year-old boy had to be taught to walk all over again, but at the end of two weeks, we were able to bring him home.

That was probably the worst time of my life. I'm a person with hardly any physical fears; I've never felt faint at the sight of the bloody mess that's almost normal on safari, and I generally tend to see the positive side of things and conveniently block out and forget what's unpleasant to remember. I don't remember any of the details, for example, of my own carotid artery operation in 1982. But having Ken or our daughters, Joan and Jerilynne, become physically sick is something I just can't take.

But we were lucky—at least, as lucky as parents could be in this kind of situation. Unlike other parents who didn't have the financial means we had or our excellent housekeeper, Virginia, both Edna and I could afford to get away from our responsibilities at home and work and spend all our time with Ken when he was in the hospital. We also could pay extra for private-duty nursing and physical therapy. Money won't buy you everything and it won't buy you health, but it helps under certain conditions. When Ken was about to be discharged, I went down to the hospital director's office because I had received no bill. The director told me that there'd be no charge since the hospital was just fulfilling its role as a public-health facility in treating a contagious disease.

"How does a guy like me say thank you?" I asked him. He thought for a minute before answering me. "There are adult polio patients here too and some of them are breadwinners. Their families are going to suffer while they're sick, so maybe you could find some way of helping them," he said.

I know that by today's standards this seems like an extraordinary suggestion from a hospital administrator, but this was before hospitals got so big and bureaucratic. Anyway, Edna began doing volunteer work with patients in iron lungs at the hospital, and we sort of adopted about five families. Every month we deposited a hundred dollars in local supermarkets for each family to draw from for groceries. We helped out with extras, like winter snowsuits for their children and holiday presents. Some children even thought I was their uncle when I came to visit their homes. A few of those families were in contact with us for about ten to twelve years after Kenny got out of the hospital until things got back to normal for them. It was an unusual form of showing appreciation to the good Lord, but one we were glad to make.

As things improved with Ken, our domestic life also brightened. Our youngest daughter, Jerilynne, was born in 1949 and made our family complete. After buying out my partner in 1948, my business expanded and thrived throughout the late 1940s and the 1950s. We had begun the Sydney Infants Wear business in 1943 as wholesalers or jobbers—buying from manufacturers at lowest prices, adding on our costs as distributors, and then selling the merchandise to individual retail stores and department-store chains. By the early 1950s, we branched out, acquired partners, and began doing some manufacturing ourselves. Then, toward the end of the decade, we found it more profitable to switch from being jobbers to sales representatives for infants' and children's wear companies, selling on a commission basis directly to major retailers. By 1959, we formed another company to do this—The Sydney Company.

One interesting perspective on the development of the infant's and children's apparel industry can be found in looking at the changes in the sales trips I made. When I started selling for Lazarus, it was literally showing my sample cases out of the trunk of an old Nash automobile I convinced my father-in-law to lend me. There was no company car then; expense accounts were held down to a bare minimum, which often meant spending the night at a local "Y" for a dollar, and there was certainly no frequent-flyer mileage on airlines.

In those early days before interstate highways and chain motels made every place look alike, funny things would happen to you on the road. I remember one sales trip out of Rochester, New York, where I got caught in a snow blizzard, veered off the road by accident, and landed off the road driving my car on a frozen lake. A man fishing through the ice waved frantically to me as I approached his canvas tent, and he directed me to a nearby house. I sat out the storm, spending five days with a widow in her farmhouse. There were no faxes then and the only phone was one we had to crank up to use, but since it was put out of order by the storm, it did me no good anyway.

For a big-city boy, I learned a lot about people when I was on the road. I met my first homosexuals and cross-dressers travelling through cities and towns in western New York State and the Midwest. The first time a homosexual made an attempted advance toward me happened after I had made a $450 sale. To celebrate, the merchandise manager was taking me out to dinner. We had just gotten into his car and were discussing where to go when all of a sudden I felt his hand on my leg. Even though I didn't want to lose the order, I made it very clear to him that I wasn't available and opened the door to leave. He apologized, I kept the sale, and we continued doing business together for many years without any further annoyances.

The wedding band I had been wearing then hadn't given me any protection, and later on it even got me in trouble when a young girl mistook it as a sign of my availability.

We were shipping piece goods to a contractor in Lancaster, Pennsylvania, who'd turn them into complete garments. Every third week or so, I'd drive to the plant to see how the production was coming, and I'd walk through the sewing department, which consisted mainly of Amish and Mennonite women and girls. Primly wearing their bonnets, they'd sit by their machines, but one day when I walked by, I noticed a lot of titters.

That night I was invited to the home of a community leader who was the father of one of the girls in the sewing department. He sent his son with a horse-and-buggy to pick me up. Over dinner, he kept referring to his daughter, Prissy, who had become smitten with me, after seeing me at the plant.

According to the practices of the particular sect she belonged to, the left hand I wore my wedding band on was a signal that I was single, so she had gotten her father to invite me home. When it became obvious that her father was talking to me as a prospective son-in-law, I immediately advised him that the ring meant I was married and certainly *not* available! In fact, I had two children already and told him that. He was very embarrassed and his ruddy face darkened and turned almost black. He immediately called a driver to take me back to town, and the girl never showed up at the plant again. Again, it took some delicate diplomacy to get out of that situation!

In contrast to those early sales trips, by the end of the 1950s, I was flying business-class to Japan where I'd be wined and dined by sales agents who enlisted *geisha* girls to help entertain prospective foreign buyers like myself.

Looking back now, I believe there were several reasons for our success: some had to do with our approach to the market and others had to do with our basic management style.

When I began in children's wear on July 16, 1935, the industry was young. Later, when my daughter Joan was born in 1940, my son Ken in 1943, and Jerilynne in 1949, I remember shopping for baby things with my wife, Edna. For each of our first two children, we could find no complete layette sets sold anywhere, so we'd go looking in different places and in different stores for sheets, diapers, safety pins, nightgowns, socks and booties, bonnets, bassinets, high chairs, potty chairs, clothing, etc.

If the customers didn't go on this item-by-item search, then the specialty shop or the department store would sometimes put the set together, but this meant labor and cost for them. I decided to manufacture complete layettes, so we'd be selling a finished product—diapers, shirts, safety pins, sheets, sleepwear—everything a mother would need to get her baby started. We were able to sell these layettes for as little as $10.95, with a luxury model retailing for $30.

We also sold bottles, sterilizers, nipples, and little things like that. It was the kind of concept that anyone with imagination and practical experience in shopping for a child could have come up with, but we were the first to do it. It was labor-saving to the customer to only have to shop in one place and for the store, which didn't have to put the package together itself. As for us, because we did the labor right in our warehouse on a mass-production basis, we were able to keep costs down so the stores were better off buying complete sets from us and selling them as a package deal. Eventually, our contracts with stores had them stocking whole sections of their infants' department with items that we wholesaled.

From this experience, we also decided to try to provide the buyer in the infants and toddlers' department with everything the customer might need for a child, whether it was outerwear, sleepwear, playwear, or underwear. After all, if we were going to work with a buyer, why not offer as many of the buyer's needs as we could?

This horizontal or blanket approach was different than the vertical structure other manufacturers used. A snowsuit manufacturer, for instance, might produce snowsuits for the infants and toddlers' size range, the 3–6 size range, and the 7–14 size range. But each of those groups required different styling, different methods of production, and then had to be sold to different buyers. By concentrating just on infants' and toddlers' wear—and we were one of the first in the industry to do so—we saved on production time and on sales time. We had to pitch to just one buyer or merchandise manager, who bought not just snowsuits from us but also sunsuits, training pants, playwear, sleepwear, and anything else that infants and toddlers could use.

Second, this horizontal approach put our company in a strong position in relation to the infants and toddlers' department of any store or chain of stores. By combining our sales staff, our products, and by concentrating our efforts into a single department, we became important to the particular merchandise manager who'd rely on us for various products. Later on, in Africa, Robert Ruark would tell me, "Use enough gun," meaning that the successful hunter changes his weapon depending on what he's going after. Here, instinctively in my business, I was using enough gun by pouring enough powder power into a single merchandising division.

Two other reasons why I've done reasonably well, both in my professional and personal life, have to do with the way I've treated people. I've always been good at building and maintaining one-on-one relationships—I feel I know how to talk to people at their own level and to make them feel comfortable with "no bull." It's a skill that's of critical importance to a salesman.

It worked to our advantage when we started as a children's wear jobber because it helped us serve one particular buyer for a long time. At that time, people would stay with companies for a long time, working their way up the ladder. We'd meet someone as a buyer; later he or she might become the merchandise manager or the administrative head of a department chain store. Over the years, we built up relationships based on trust—our customers knew the kind of product they'd be getting from us, knew they'd get it on time, and knew they were getting their money's worth. In turn, we knew what kinds of orders we could expect from them.

But these days someone can be in the store buying infants' wear for two weeks and then be transferred to the shoe department and then two or three months later, the person might be involved in the insurance division of the company. So there's no continuity or chance to build up those kinds of one-on-one relationships today.

Another reason for our success has been my luck in finding the right people to work with—not just because of the skills they had but because of the loyalty and respect we had for each other. In over forty-five years of business, I've only had six partners within four distinct businesses and there was no relationship between the businesses or the partners. Each partner's connection was only to me, yet there used to be a joke among us that if I sneezed they got pneumonia!

Another example of loyalty with business associates is the fact that I've had only two secretaries— the first, Gert, was with me for twenty-four years and then Phyllis Paynter worked with me for twenty-one years. They say that no one knows a businessman better than his secretary, so the record of these two remarkable women must say something. Phyllis, especially, became loved by my whole family and she was a valuable asset to me—smart and able to anticipate my every need. There were many other employees also who were with our companies for many years and contributed to our success.

At home, we were also lucky with our employees. Our housekeeper, Virginia Carter, was with us for almost thirty years and was greatly responsible for bringing up our three children. A wonderful lady who became part of our family, she had come to us from a seminary in South Carolina. When she died we buried her and to this day, many years after her death, we maintain and visit her cemetery plot.

Edward Thomas also worked for us for many years both at home and by driving me to the office sometimes. This gave me a chance to plan my day's work or to get some paperwork done in the car. He'd then work in the office a bit until it was time to drive home. Edward was a devout Baptist, and through him I got interested in the things his church did for the black community. In appreciation for my helping them out sometimes, Edward's minister, Reverend Days, made me an honorary Deacon of their church.

I believe I get along well with people partly because of my personality. I respect people, whether it's the man who shines my shoes or the chairman of a Dow Jones corporation. In fact, I probably treat the shoe-shiner with more respect because he's doing a job I don't want to do.

I also always look on the bright side and expect the

best of people. Because I expect good things, I usually get them. I chose business associates, for example, who were capable not just of carrying their load, but mine too at times and they did when I went on safaris to Africa almost every eighteen months from the late 1950s to 1980.

My attitude toward people was also partly shaped by my conscious decision never to treat anyone the way I saw my first boss treat his workers. He was a tough and unbending person who ran things his way only; if things went wrong, he'd call you on the carpet and berate you without caring who else was present.

I was lucky enough, though, to have an Uncle George who worked with me for many years and kept me from ever acting like my first boss, whom he had known. In fact, Uncle George died in 1991 at ninety-four years of age. He was my mother's brother with a crackerjack knowledge of production. But he also reminded me how unpleasant Lazarus had been, whenever I came dangerously close to acting like him. Most situations, Uncle George believed, could be solved just by sitting and thinking out the problem in a positive way rather than by getting hot under the collar. Although I didn't have to use him too often, in a way you could say he was my in-company psychologist.

My management style was also different from my first employer's. From the start of my own business, I knew that it had to be departmentalized, no matter how small it might be. It had to be put into categories—selling, administration, production, shipping, accounting, etc. They say that an entrepreneur or the boss has to know all the jobs of a company and, to a degree, that's true. But I soon discovered that people know their

Sydney Jarkow at age five

The author in 1959, announcing the formation of the Sydney Company

A successful display set up in major department stores of preprinted names of boys and girls on polo shirts

Sydney Infants Wear Inc. sales and managerial staff about 1952

About mid-1950, being entertained in Osaka, Japan, as a customer; eventually we produced only in the U.S.A.

Sydney Jarkow about age forty-five in his New York office

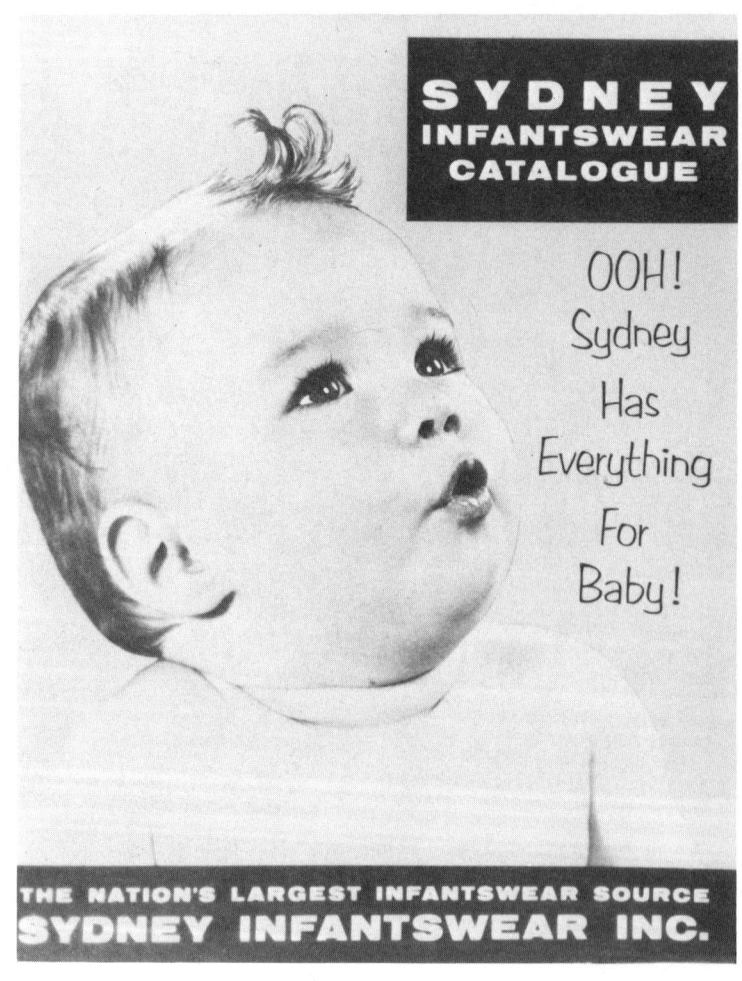

The cover of a thirty-four-page catalogue of the author's wholesale division

A prize sailfish caught off the coast of Mexico

Edna and Sydney, early 1950s

individual jobs better and can do them faster and more economically then I ever could.

I learned to departmentalize my company and delegate responsibility. Because of that, I threw responsibilities onto people and then stood back. Most of the time, they accomplished what I was looking for in them, so I then went on to give them more responsibility. This worked out wonderfully. My employees were happy because I trusted and respected them. It also made it easier for me. It especially gave me the time I needed away from business, which became very important to me once I started travelling for business and going on safaris and family vacations.

But I was never an absentee kind of boss. It had been my policy to keep key employees constantly charged up or alert and on the watch for products that would fit into our type of operation, which had quickly expanded into some manufacturing as well as wholesaling other manufacturers' goods. That's why I instructed my staff that my office, telephone, and home were always open and available to them.

Early in 1950 that policy really paid off when I got a phone call in the middle of the night from Tony, one of my production people at a Lancaster, Pennsylvania, plant. Tony was a new father who had been warming up his baby's 2:00 A.M. feeding when he dropped the glass bottle on the floor where it shattered. While Tony was mopping up the mess, he noticed a plastic bottle containing deodorant sitting on the shelf, and he thought that if the baby bottle was made of the same material, the mess wouldn't have happened.

Tony called me at 2:30 A.M. to tell me he thought baby bottles should be made of unbreakable material. While I was initially annoyed to receive a call at that hour, I reminded myself that I had always told my employees I was available to them and that I should be grateful Tony responded the way he did.

I made some bedside notations for a shatter-proof baby bottle and the next morning when I got into the office, I called in my assistant, Alan Stuart. He's a prime example of my ability to find the right person for the job. Alan was older than I was and had been Dean of Men at Hofstra University on Long Island. When I had met him a year earlier, he was thinking of leaving the college world because he wasn't making enough money. By 1950, my business had grown to the point where I needed someone with the educational background I did not possess—someone also with an eye for details who could help put all my plans into action. Hiring worked out well for both of us.

At that time, baby bottles were made of glass and they were really products of the drug field. I put the task of finding an unbreakable baby bottle into Alan's hands. We were both new fathers, so we knew the bottle had to be sterilized in order to be used by an infant. Up until that time, I knew of no plastic bottle that could be sterilized without melting out of shape. Alan set out the next morning to find a plant that could make the kind of material without telling them what it would be used for.

Most polyethylene plants were in the Midwest, and Alan travelled to seven of them, calling in to report after each visit, before finding one in Prescott, Arizona, that could meet our needs. It was a major expenditure for our company, but we figured it would be worthwhile. While he was out looking for a source of supply, I was busy with patent attorneys and we tied up every bottle shape and size that could be useful to the infants' industry.

It cost us about $85,000 finally to produce the bottle after going through many trials. We soon discovered that we couldn't properly market the bottle because 97 percent of baby bottles were sold in drug stores and the balance in other outlets. We'd have to neglect our regular trade to put our efforts into another industry, so I decided to find a major distributor and work on a royalty basis.

Several drug companies were excited with the product, and I finally chose a major outfit that had been in business for 106 years and had a record for success. The deal was that they'd use their own manufacturing facilities and our patent, for which they'd pay us $.32 per dozen with a gradual increase after the initial advertising and promotion costs, which the distributor would absorb.

Sales started reasonably well and before we knew it, we were making $50,000–$60,000 plus in royalties. By our fourth year, we had earned about a total of $400,000 in royalties, but our luck was short-lived because after five years of association, this company filed for bankruptcy.

As things worked out, I learned a major lesson about business from this. Our contract had been so badly written by the attorneys that no provision was made for the patent to revert back to us in case of bankruptcy. I can only blame myself for not having been more careful about the contents of a legal contract; I also learned that attorneys, like all other professionals, should be checked for a second opinion. But I have no real complaint because we made considerable amounts of money over our cost of producing that bottle.

I relied on Alan, not just for help with the baby bottle, but to assist me in implementing other business innovations as well. We were the first infants' and children's wear company to issue an illustrated catalog of all our merchandise, and Alan did all the designing and copy writing for that. It worked as a great sales tool to leave with buyers. Another simple but innovative sales tool Alan helped me design was the sales rack. Prior to its introduction, merchandise was just piled high on tables. With the wire rack, packaged small items like socks or underwear could be displayed to customers much more visibly and effectively.

As I've said, when the Sydney Infants Wear Company began, we were a wholesale company catering to small children's wear retailers. But by the late 1940s to the early 1950s, the industry was changing and so was our company. I soon discovered that the real growth and strength of children's wear was in the large department and chain stores like Sears, J.C. Penney, and eventually K-Mart and later Wal-Mart. As wholesalers, we were not positioned advantageously to sell to the big retailers, so I decided to approach some of our suppliers to allow us to sell their products directly to these companies on a commission basis.

My first connection with this new adventure was with Alpha Mills, which had been supplying us with infants' knitted underwear and playwear from a plant in Schuylkil Haven, Pennsylvania. The company, owned by the Biever family, traded only with wholesalers and operated on a very small margin of profit. The ninety-three-year-old grandfather, his son, and grandson ran the business, but they were more interested in running their dairy farm and raising black Angus cattle.

Our relationship was very good, and they gave full cooperation in my plan to act as their sales representative. With the connections and sales tools available to us, we developed such a strong demand for their production that after the second year of my association, they gave me a small interest. I remember joining them for lunch to sign the contract; then, as we walked outside, a big, shiny Cadillac sedan drew up. "It's a reward for your work, Sydney," they told me.

That was my first luxury car, and I remember how proud I felt driving home to Long Island in it and what a sensation it made on our street in 1955. It was quite a change from the old Nash my father-in-law had reluctantly lent me to make my early sales trips in. Twenty years later, Edna and I bought our first Rolls Royce to satisfy her early dreams, and we still drive one today, but I'll never forget that first Cadillac.

While we were spending more time as sales representatives, we were also still running the wholesale company and that continued to do well. Having set a pattern for ourselves and having been accepted as a reliable source of supply by the major department-store chains, we continued to find other companies to form joint ventures and partnerships with. One of these business associations became formalized as Pixie Playmates in 1954. It blossomed into a close relationship between two brothers and myself and still continues today in both our families through our sons.

It began when our wholesale company first started to buy inexpensive infant and toddler playwear from Harold Lopatin's small manufacturing plant in Brooklyn. As with our earlier association with the Biever knitwear plant in Pennsylvania, we positioned ourselves to sell to the major chain stores by having Lopatin's company work for us on a contract basis. Under that arrangement, we purchased the piece goods from the mills, shipped them to the factory in Brooklyn, which then made the finished garments and shipped them to our warehouse. They would charge us for labor, and their profit would be added on to the price.

We soon found out that in order to be a real competitive factor in our industry, we could cut our costs by putting both our companies together, and so Pixie Playmates was born in 1954 and relocated to a small plant in Tarpon Springs, Florida. After about five years, it moved to Largo, Florida, and became one of the largest factories manufacturing garments in Florida. Although Sydney Infants Wear continued to add other companies to our small conglomerate, the Pixie Playmate division became one of my favorites because of the mutual affectionate relationship that existed between the Lopatin brothers and myself.

While my business was growing and prospering during the 1950s, so was my family. Dinner and my children may have had to wait as late as 7:30 P.M. sometimes for me to come home, but when I came home, I was truly home. Rarely, if ever, did I bring business talk or paperwork home with me on the evenings or weekends. If I knew how to work hard, I also knew how to play hard and I enjoyed my children's company. It was me, not Edna, who took Joan, our oldest daughter, clothing shopping, even for her high school prom dresses. Edna and I socialized a lot with a group of friends called "The Kitty Club," since we all put money into a kitty so we could go out big sometimes. But I always made it a point to spend time with each of my children separately before going out at night.

We went on family vacations together, and sometimes I'd take shorter trips with each child alone. I remember hunting quail and pheasant with Ken when he was around twelve years old, taking Joan on a train trip to Miami and teaching her to eat oysters, and going with Jerilynne on shorter trips. Edna and I also travelled on our own. One trip to Cuba was fun because it was the first time in my life I was mistaken for a movie star.

Edna and I and a group of our friends had gone to a night spot on the outskirts of Havana that was like a nickel-a-dance joint. We wanted to mix with the Cuban people, and we were having fun dancing Cuban-style and changing partners with everyone.

All of a sudden, some Cuban girls gathered around me saying, "Ameche, Ameche." I didn't know what they were talking about—there was a large twenty-piece orchestra playing; it was a big hall with lots of noise and people, and more and more of them were surrounding me. The manager finally made his way to me through the crowd and said in a mixture of Spanish and English, "Ameche, Ameche, give them your autograph."

At the time, I was well-tanned, with thick black hair, and I had a neatly trimmed mustache. I was wearing a white suit and I guess I looked pretty good, good enough for these Cuban girls to confuse me with Don Ameche, a movie star in the 1940s and 1950s who acted in romantic comedies. I tried telling the manager that I wasn't Don Ameche, but he didn't seem to understand and the crowd kept getting larger and larger. Finally, one of the guys with us said, "Just tell them you are Ameche, sign your autograph, and let's get out of here." So I started signing napkins, their white *cubavera* jackets, or anything they had, and finally the local militia came and eased us out of there.

But if I was mistaken for Don Ameche when I was young, as I've aged and my hair and mustache have whitened, people have confused me with Douglas Fairbanks, Jr. In fact, Edna and I used to have a New York City apartment on Fifth Avenue and Sixty-first Street, and Fairbanks lived nearby on about Madison Avenue and Sixty-second Street. Every once in a while, we'd run into each other and nod, and one time his wife stopped me and said, "You know, you and my husband must have been brothers." I thanked her and we chatted for a while and after that whenever Fairbanks and I ran into each other, we'd wave and say, "Hello, brother."

But back to business—by the end of the 1950s, two trends changed the nature of our company. The first was information I received from a friend who worked as a buyer for J.C. Penney. According to him, the major department and discount chains were going to cut costs by ordering merchandise through sales representatives rather than buying from wholesalers or jobbers. Because the jobber is an indirect source of supply who buys the merchandise and then ships it out to stores, he has to add in his costs and profits. But a sales representative acts on a commission basis, which means he can do well while the retailers can still buy direct from the manufacturers.

Since we were doing more sales than jobbing anyway, we formed the Sydney Company in 1959. It would act as the sales arm of the parent company

Sydney Infants Wear and as the sales representative for other manufacturers of children's wear.

Another new development was the trend for American textile and garment businesses to move their production facilities to the Orient or to Caribbean islands in order to take advantage of cheap labor costs. We too began importing some of our production from the Far East and other parts of the world where labor was sometimes as low as 32 cents an hour. By comparison, by 1955 American workers were earning a minimum wage of $1.00 an hour.

Although I made many visits to Japan, Hong Kong, and islands in the South Pacific, truthfully I never enjoyed those trips as much as I loved going to Africa. The Far East just didn't have the lure for me that Africa did, and I was glad to turn over a lot of our Far Eastern business to my son, Ken, when he came to work for us full-time. Incidentally, as time went on, business with the Far East became more complicated; shipments were delayed; orders became misplaced, and it became more difficult to do business long-distance. Just as we were one of the first to do business outside of America, we also became one of the first to pull back and resume doing all our production in the United States. Through sophisticated manufacturing methods, we were able to be competitive with Hong Kong, Taiwan, Haiti, and other low-cost labor countries and we were very proud to display huge tags on our garments saying "Made in the U.S.A."

During most of the 1950s, my family, my business interests, and American society, in general, grew and thrived. Transistor radios, Polaroid cameras, and miracle drugs were discovered; Americans moved in masses to suburbs and shopped at discount store chains; canasta and hula hoops were big fads; and worldwide credit cards became widely available although I've only used them sparingly in my personal life.

The 1950s weren't all wonderful—there was the Korean War, the U.S. House Un-American Activities hearings, and other wars in Algeria and Indochina. But overall, there seemed to be an expansive feeling to the decade that anything was possible. Space exploration was just beginning, and a thirty-four-year-old beekeeper from New Zealand named Edmund P. Hillary had climbed twenty-nine thousand feet to the top of Mount Everest, the world's highest mountain.

In my own way, I had climbed mountains also. I was well-respected in business and in my social community; I was materially successful and had a happy and healthy family. My children, friends, and employees always found me ready and willing to listen to them while my relatives found me willing to lend a hand and share my success with them. I say this, not to boast, but simply as the way I behaved. I won't even say I did it all for altruistic reasons but just because it was part of my personality—the way I had turned over my earnings to my parents when I was twelve years old.

But now, it was time to grow and to challenge myself still further. So I decided to live out a dream I had had for a long time and to go to Africa on safari.

Chapter Three
Africa—The First Safari

I never had a bar mitzvah—the religious ceremony that marks a Jewish boy's transition to manhood at age thirteen. But it's an interesting coincidence that I began to plan how to fulfill a long-time dream to go on an African safari in my thirteenth year of business. Maybe in an odd sort of way, I used the safari as my own coming-of-age ritual.

I started thinking seriously about Africa in 1956. By that time, my business was well enough established for me to leave it in the hands of trusted partners and employees; my three children aged sixteen, thirteen, and eight were old enough for me to leave in the good hands of my wife; and I had had my first real taste of decent money.

After years of building a business, of taking care of my aging parents and helping my brothers and their families while also starting a family of my own, I think I had just reached the point where I was comfortable enough—financially and emotionally—to feel I could get away for a time. It seemed the right time to try to make one of my dreams come true, and to me an African safari was the greatest adventure of them all.

Now, I grew up in Brooklyn, New York, and made my living in the Garment District. While some might say those experiences can prepare you for surviving in a jungle, I can't say honestly that I remember anything in my background actually preparing me for Africa.

Sure, I had read adventure stories featuring the Rover Boys as a kid, I had looked at *National Geographic* magazines in the public library, and I had seen Tarzan movies, but I was a boy from a middle-class background who grew up to become a comfortable, respected businessman and family man.

If I had any role model at all for going to hunt big game in Africa, it was John Pirie, the chairman of Carson, Pirie, and Scott, a major Midwestern department-store chain. He was about forty years older than I was when we first met in the late 1930s. I was in Chicago on a sales trip for my boss, A. S. Lazarus, and had talked a buyer into seeing my sample case of clothes even though it was a Saturday. On Saturdays, buyers were supposed to be out on the floor managing the sales staff, not seeing traveling salesmen, but I didn't know that and, besides, I was going to be leaving town later that afternoon.

I had just begun my sales pitch when Mr. Pirie came up behind me. Instead of reprimanding the buyer, Mr. Pirie also started looking at my merchandise. After listening patiently to why I had made what we call a "cold call" rather than phoning first for an appointment to show my line, he said, "Carry on, young man, and come up to my office when you're done here."

I remember taking the elevator up to see him and wondering if he was going to tell me not to come back to his store ever again. I felt as if I were going up to an ivory tower. The man was looked up to by everyone, and his office was as impressive as you'd expect for a man of his position.

What I noticed most was that it was filled with the heads of big-game trophies he had shot. I could see he wasn't just the administrator of a huge business but a man who also took time to enjoy the world. He saw me staring at the heads on his walls and asked if I was interested in the sport of hunting. I said no but the germ of the idea must have been planted in my imagination because whenever I went back to see him on later sales trips, we'd talk about Africa and he promised to arrange a safari for me when I was ready.

It was to him that I turned for advice after first discussing my plans with Edna. Her attitude was very reasonable, I thought. "You can go to Africa by yourself because all you'll see there are animals," she said, "but you'd better not go off to Grossinger's alone because that's where the big game is men and women on the prowl for each other." (At that time, Grossinger's, a hotel in New York's Catskill Mountain range, had a reputation for its "fun and games.")

Mr. Pirie helped me contact Philip Percival who, at that time, was the dean of all white hunters—"highly respected and a perfect gentleman" was how Pirie described him. And, indeed, when I first met him in British East Africa, which was where Kenya Colony was located in 1958, he looked as though he had stepped straight out of Hollywood's Central Casting Office—he was tall, thin, and imposing-looking in a weather-beaten way.

Percival himself had retired from professional hunting although he still kept a pack of dogs and used them to hunt wart hog and the occasional leopard that wandered onto his farm outside Nairobi. But he turned me over to one of the best safari outfitters, Safariland, Ltd. You don't just fly to Africa and hire a white hunter the way you can rent a car and book a travel guide on a day's notice.

There are only about seventy-five licensed big-game hunters in all of Africa. Their services are sometimes booked a year or two in advance because you can only go out certain times of the year, depending on the kind of game you want. But it's worth the wait because the success of your safari often depends on your hunter.

First of all, you're literally putting your life in his hands, since the primary role of the professional hunter is to back up the client—you—in dangerous situations. But you also have to trust the hunter to know the land, to know the favorite haunts and habits of the game you're after, and how to set the right pace.

You count on him to communicate with the African staff, and his personality sets the tone for the safari—whether he's friendly or aloof, hot-tempered or even-handed with the staff, comfortable to be with or not. After all, you're going to be travelling with him for weeks at a time, with little or no outsiders for diversions. I guess I'm lucky because in a little more than twenty-two years of going on safari, I've only had one hunter I didn't like.

Through letters, spaced out over weeks, we established the kind of "bag" or game I wanted to secure—odd, now that I think about it, that game hunters talk in terms of "securing" or "filling" a bag rather than shooting or killing animals. I had shot some birds and small game, like rabbits and deer, in upstate New York and Canada, but I had never gone after any rougher stuff, such as big cats or bear. In Africa, I wanted to try for all the exotic big game, but I decided to leave it in the hands of the experts at Safariland.

Once we settled that, other things fell into place, especially the best time of the year to go on safari, which had to depend not only on my business schedule but on local African weather conditions as well. The best time to go on safari is just when the rainy season is finishing and the dry season starts. During the rains, grass grows abundantly and the game feeds very well. Then as you get into the dry season, conditions improve for hunting and you have a better chance for spotting animals because they come to gather at whatever water holes are available.

During this planning stage, I had talked to friends and business associates about coming with me. Although many of them thought the idea of Africa sounded exciting, only one of them, Gerry, was really serious about wanting to go. Gerry had his own automobile agency in New Jersey. He had a wife but no children, and he went to Africa more on a lark than as the fulfillment of a dream as I did. Although he was eager to go, he really let me put all the details together for our adventure and was a great companion.

It took two years of planning before we finally got to Africa on November 22, 1958. I was forty-three years old when I stepped out of the BOAC turbo prop onto the tarmac at Khartoum and felt the hot, dry desert air of the Sudan. The Arabic-speaking Muslim natives were dressed in long white gowns and wore white turbans. Even the Sudanese officers were all in white, and it was like seeing something out of a Rudyard Kipling story or a Foreign Legion movie. After months of paperwork, of setting my business and professional affairs in order, of exercising a lot to get into good physical shape and getting a whole series of shots to prevent tropical diseases, I was finally close to the African safari adventure I had long dreamed of!

In those days, even air travel took time—we had spent more than a day getting from New York to North

Africa, with stops in London and Rome for refueling, and now we'd spend the night in Khartoum before taking off the next morning for Uganda and then Kenya, our final destination.

It wasn't until we flew into the tiny, tin-roofed airport in Entebbe, a true outpost in the midst of jungle, that I got my first whiff of that real heavy, moist air that you find only in the tropics. In comparison, the modern airport at Nairobi seemed almost anticlimatic.

After spending the night in a downtown Nairobi hotel, Gerry and I were met the next morning by our two professional hunters—Bill Jenvey and Bill Morkel. Both were cast out of the same mold—suntanned, well-built, and well-informed young men. Jenvey, who was going to be my hunter, was the more experienced of the two—a slight, wiry guy. I'd go on later safaris with him while Morkel eventually gave up professional hunting to become a farmer.

Gerry and I were anxious to get started, imagining the wild game that waited for us less than an hour from town. On some nights, if the wind was right, you could still hear hyenas, the staff at the hotel had told us. But first there were final details to discuss—how many men to hire and how much equipment, food, and liquor we'd have to bring for a three-week safari. (Looking at my old bills shows that in all that time Gerry and I and our two hunters went through less than two bottles of whiskey!) We also needed to settle what kind of guns and ammo we'd needed from the outfitters, since we were advised not to bring our own. In fact, on these early safaris, I only brought one serviceable gun with me, a .306 caliber rifle. Guns were never that important to me; in between safaris I hardly ever practiced shooting.

Above all, there was the matter of licenses to buy. In Kenya, even in the 1950s, the type of big game you could legally hunt and the area you could hunt in were strictly controlled by licensing. In 1958, for example, only two hundred hunting licenses were sold in all of Kenya. Your license spelled out where you could hunt, what you could hunt, and how much you could hunt. Sometimes you got the permits you wanted; other times you didn't. On that first safari, for instance, I missed a chance to bag a rhino we unexpectedly came across because he wasn't on my license. Nor could you go outside your hunting area to follow an animal's spoor or track unless it was to finish him off or unless he was threatening human life.

Gerry and I also had to get personally outfitted for the safari. We had been told to bring nothing but toiletries, some personal items, and a few very old clothes, so our hunters took us to an Arab-owned store where we were measured for bush jackets, shorts, shirts, and boots. Interestingly, we learned why bush clothes are basically tan or green: bright colors like yellow, white, or red not only make the wildlife alert to their glare, but they also attract insects.

Our clothes were ready the next day, and we also bought heavy sweaters to wear at night. Although the equator runs through Kenya, making the sun strong and hot during the day, at night the temperature drops by as much as twenty degrees sometimes because of high altitudes. Nairobi, for example, lying high on a plateau, is nearly six thousand feet high.

Four days after we had first landed in Africa, we set out for the game preserves that had been set aside for us. In addition to our two hunters, we travelled with about two dozen Wakamba tribesmen and some men from different tribes who would act as gun-bearers, trackers, porters, cooks, skinners, and other helpers who were called "camp boys" by everyone at the time even though they were all men.

Our destination was the highland country of southwestern Kenya. Located on either side of Norok, nothing more than a Masai trading post near the Tanganyika border, reserve #57 was a thousand square miles and reserve #59 covered two thousand miles. I learned on that first safari that the most sporting way to track and kill game is on foot, a practice I followed up to my last safari. But at times while we were crisscrossing that territory, Gerry and I joked that our feet felt as if they had walked over more land than either Stanley or Livingstone.

The first morning in camp, Gerry and I woke before sunrise, ate breakfast, and set off separately with our own hunters and gun-bearers. I felt as if I had finally arrived where I most wanted to be, but I also felt a sense of trepidation—"Jesus Christ, now that I'm really here, I'm going to have to go through it."

It's just overwhelmingly open out there in the bush with no separation between you and the game—no bars, fences, or moats. Just the professional hunter to back you up and the realization of that hits hard. So anyone who says they're not afraid when they're hunting a predatory animal or something large like a Cape buffalo is just a cockeyed liar!

But tracking game that first day, I was also aware of being in some of the most beautiful country I could ever hope to see. It was hilly and rough going at times, but there were also yellow-flowered acacia trees; thick-trunked, upside-down baobob trees, which look as if their roots are where the branches normally would be;

ocher-colored clay on the ground, which I later found out the Masai used to paint their bodies; and the red and green hills of Kenya. Above it all, an endless canopy of unbroken blue sky. Of course, almost all of my perceptions, during this time, were affected by a feeling of intoxication—I think I was simply drunk with the whole idea of being on safari and being where I was.

Almost every day we'd see a parade of wildlife—baboons, impala, eland, "Tommies," as I learned to call Thompson's gazelles, wildebeest, wart hogs, bat-eared foxes, and dik diks, the smallest of all antelopes, no larger than a large hare and among the most difficult to shoot because of their dainty size and ability to hide in the tall grass. It was remarkable to be actually able to spot the game and then track the spoor—the footprints, droppings, and other markings left by the passing animal. It was what I had come a long way to do, what I had prepared for, and now that I was actually doing it, I felt a real sense of accomplishment and boundless energy.

Now, to be a success in business, you have to have a certain kind of natural alertness—to people and the cues around you. Here in Africa I was alert in a different way—to the natural world around me—and I think my ability to use my senses sharply to be a good stalker came out to the fullest in Africa.

On my first day out, I bagged two Tommies—golden animals the size of a pointer dog with black bars on their faces—a zebra, and an impala, suggesting to Bill Jenvey that I was probably an instinctive shooter. Now I had hunted rabbit, birds, and other small game at home and most of the time had always felt some burst of emotion when I had been successful. But it was nothing to compare with what I felt in Africa. At times,

I felt exhilarated—almost hilarious with joy; other times, such as on a later safari when I had to put a wounded elephant out of his misery—he had been illegally shot with poison darts by some natives—I felt extremely depressed.

But back on that first safari, there were more good feelings than anything else. Our lives were pretty simple: hunting, talking, and trading with local Masai in their *manyattas* or villages, eating, and sleeping.

Typically, we'd be awakened at 4:30 A.M. by a black head peering in our tent, saying "*Chai* [tea], *bwana, chai.*" We'd eat breakfast and leave camp at about 5:30 A.M. just when the sun would start to break through. Gerry and I would go off and hunt separately, meeting back at the camp in the evenings. If my hunter and I weren't on the spoor of an animal and trailing it, we'd try to find our way back to camp for lunch. Then we might go back out to the bush in the late afternoon.

But more often than not, if we were out in the bush and there was no forest cover around us, we'd walk back to the Land Rover, have a simple lunch of canned beans, fruit, and crackers, and crawl next to or under the car for shade. If we were on the spoor of an animal, especially if it was a predator or looked like a trophy animal, we'd just stay on the trail and skip eating all together.

Generally, we'd be back in camp sometime between 5:00 and 7:00 P.M. because it would get real dark by then; we'd bathe, change, and meet over the campfire to have some beer or whiskey and talk about the day's events. Camp life was pretty sedate actually because you can't drink a lot in the evening and still be able to get up and go hunting before sunrise. On safari you need to have all your wits about you and being hung-over instead of clear-headed and alert could be the difference between life and death. We usually turned in by 9:00 P.M. and after a while, I adopted the professional hunter's trick of changing into the clothes I'd wear the next day, instead of sleeping in pajamas, so I'd save time in the morning. Besides, it kept me warmer during the night.

A daily log I kept on that safari shows how much Gerry and I wanted to take a lion and a leopard. The Masai had told us the predators were in the area, so we spent a lot of time hunting for bait and checking the blinds we had built.

Sunday, November 30, 1958
... by 8:30 A.M., I got three zebras and by 12:30 P.M. got a wildebeest. We strung two of the zebras and the wildebeest up for bait in various places and built blinds for leopard and lion, which took about four hours to build. Tracked buffalo in the afternoon but didn't see any. Inspected the bait we set up earlier and did not get back to camp until 8:00 P.M. Dinner and bed. A good day.

Monday, December 1, 1958
Started out real early. Got up at 4:00 A.M. to be at the blinds before daybreak. No nibble. This is most intense. You die a thousand deaths approaching the bait in the dark in anticipation of coming on to a lion or leopard.

Reading those entries now, I see what a master of understatement I was—walking out in the pitch darkness to see if a lion or leopard was waiting for you or even just doing twelve hours of hard walking during the day. Wow! It's probably good that I didn't know what I was in for beforehand.

Tuesday, December 2, 1958
Up at 4:30 to approach blinds. The zebra and wildebeest were nibbled at, but no sign of leopard or lion. We'll try again.

Walked up a mountain about 9,500 feet high, looking for a buffalo again. No sign of any; however, walking through the woods, spotted a rhino about fifty to sixty yards from us. If we had a license to take one, I would have gotten it for sure. Took pictures instead—when it heard the click, it started out for us, then stopped suddenly. Must have walked five miles today over hill and dale. The altitude here is very high and both Gerry and I find we get tired fast, especially when walking uphill.

Back for lunch in camp about 1:00 P.M. and then started out for the blinds again to try to catch them [the leopard or lion] at their evening meal. Lay in wait for two hours and fifteen minutes *without moving!* No luck. Picked up four guinea hens on the way back—three with one shot.

I wasn't lucky that day, but Gerry was. He came back to camp with a beautiful leopard he had shot, and that evening the boys carried him around camp on a chair for celebration. He was delighted and I was happy for him. It would take me several more days and hours of waiting motionlessly and patiently before I spotted a leopard, but although I got off one good shot, it wasn't the "killing shot." Bill Jenvey finished it off with a buckshot blast. I'd get my own victory celebration on another safari.

During that trip, however, we also got our full share

of plains game—impala, zebra, different gazelles, hartebeest, and wildebeest. Even though the shooting was great, after a while we passed up a great deal of game because it didn't make sense to shoot the animals if we didn't need any more of them for trophies. We also got to see elephant and rhino and came close to buffalo but decided to give it up because the conditions weren't right. Since we were getting more into the dry season, the only place to find buffalo was in the heavily wooded areas near the streams and that was dangerous because it left us no room for escape if the animal started to charge us.

Most evenings, tucked inside our tents, we could also hear a starlit symphony of animal sounds—the howling of hyenas, the hoarse coughs of a lion, occasionally a strange barking sound, which turned out to be zebra, the shrill chatter of baboons, and the steady, sawing sound of a leopard. One night, we camped right across a river, which was only knee high, from a pride of lions. Later, we could see their eyes shine as we lay in bed. I'll never forget that!

If being out in the open bush during the daytime gave me a sense of being in thrilling but potentially dangerous contact with animals, the thin cloth of our tents at night was only a symbolic barrier between me and them. But still I wouldn't trade lying on a creaky, narrow camp bed under a canvas roof in the middle of the African night for the most four-star accommodations.

Unless we were going to be staying in a camp for only a brief time, most of the time we enjoyed the luxury of a classic "Manyara" tent. It was made of heavy-duty canvas, supported by tall, thick poles, and secured by long guy ropes and stout tent pegs. Designed in two layers—an inner and outer tent, separated by two feet—this old-fashioned style offered all the comforts you could expect to find in the bush—relative coolness in hot weather, lots of roominess (it was about eight feet high), and safety from predators, snakes, and insects.

Other times and on different safaris, I stayed in lightweight tents that eliminated the need for big support poles and awkward guy ropes because of their modern, streamlined design. But even those were big enough to stand up and move around in. Both styles of tents were shaded outside by an awning, so if we were back in camp after lunch, we'd spend the midday there out of the sun catching up on reading or writing letters.

This first safari seemed pretty rugged to me and not a pampered, luxury trip. But even so, we each had our own tents and a tent boy whose responsibility was to bring each of us tea in the morning, to do our laundry and iron our sheets during the day, and to hang up a canvas bag on a wooden frame, which had been filled with 102-degree water for your bath when you returned from hunting. Sometimes, they'd just punch holes in a large can, climb up above you, and it would be a crude shower. I never found out why, but I noticed on most safaris that the camp boys wore long white robes, suggesting that they were Muslims.

Toilets were pretty basic, though—generally, "drop holes" located about ten to fifteen yards from our tents. They were about two feet deep and covered with some wooden planks for you to squat on. One of the few luxury items we always packed was enough toilet paper, but even then we used it sparingly.

Maybe because they knew we were novices, the two

hunters and the staff did try to give us as much comfort as they could. I remember the cook baking a cake one night in an old tin trunk set over coals. Earlier in the day, I had mentioned it was my eldest daughter's birthday.

But most of the time, the food didn't vary that much. Breakfast would usually consist of tea and some kind of cracker or flatbread the cook had been able to make on the fire; lunch in camp would be cold meat from what we had hunted the day before and fresh fruit if we were able to barter for it; and then dinner would be something out of maize, whatever game we had shot for the pot, and vegetables and fruit depending on their availability. Lots of times we also filled in on canned and dry goods like beans and rice. In most cases, the table would be set with candles, not for romance, but to save whatever kerosene we had.

For everything—supplies, food and lodging, and everyone's daily fees—I once figured that the first safari cost me approximately $85–90 a day. The last hunt I took in 1980 cost me $1,125 a day.

After arranging for P. Zimmermann, an internationally known taxidermist, to transport our trophies home, we had some free time to spare once we got back to Nairobi. One of the hunters suggested if we wanted a close look at the way life in old East Africa used to be like, we should go down to the coast on the Indian Ocean. So we chartered a private plane and flew to Malindi, a small Arab fishing village. Both Africans and Arabs lived there, and it was an interesting mix of people.

We swam in the ocean, visited native markets, which were both colorful and primitive, and generally hung out and relaxed—something we needed after the long hours on safari. It wasn't just the physical activity that had been draining, but when you're on safari, all your mental energy is focussed on the hunt. You're always alert, always concentrating on what's around you, and that's tiring.

Because of this, I found some kind of decompression time before returning to my "real life" back home. On later trips, I usually arranged in advance to spend this kind of time with Edna in a more modern or European city. It was a good way to ease back into the role of being a responsible business and family man.

But for now it was still the guys having one last fling at doing something wild (by Long Island standards). We even went farther down the coast to Mombasa, a port town that seemed to belong in a Grade B, black-and-white Hollywood movie. One night we visited a real low-down seaport joint where some young Scandinavian sailors on leave danced with African girls. Of course, they were there to get laid, but being respectable, married men, Gerry and I just watched and tried to guess who'd go home with whom.

Gerry and I flew home a few days later on a large, beautiful Pan Am 707 jet we had caught in London. It was quite a change from the small Piper Comanche we chartered to fly us to Mombasa—more comfortable, yes, but not as thrilling as flying over the green African mountains and plains.

On reflection now, maybe that contrast represents the attraction that Africa had come to hold for me because I knew upon leaving that I would return. Gerry had come for the excitement of going to Africa; I had come because I wanted to go on an adventure. The difference between us was that having gotten the excitement, Gerry was satisfied, but once I got a taste of the adventure that was possible in Africa, I became determined to somehow make it a part of my life.

On one side, there was the materially comfortable, predictable life I led back home: I was a pillar of my suburban community, a respectable golfer, an experienced businessman, the man everyone seemed to look to for advice. Then, there was Africa—full of the unknown, the challenge and risk of testing myself physically and mentally, and just plain excitement.

I had satisfied some of my initial curiosity about Africa with this first trip, but it only made me curious to see more. I had begun to learn about different tribespeople on this trip, to understand what being a hunter or stalker really meant, and I intended to continue seeing more of the continent on future safaris.

Chapter Four
Returning to Africa Again and Again

I began preparing for my second safari about eight months after I came home from my first one. I knew almost immediately that I was going to return to Africa, not just because of the thrill of the sport of hunting, but because being in Africa had somehow taken me out of the world. It wasn't just a matter of camping out in the bush with no barriers between me and the game, which I found exciting, but getting to know the hunters and the Africans had taken me out of my normal way of life and introduced me to people and life-styles I hadn't been able to imagine before.

But first there was a new business at home to attend to. I had started Sydney Infants Wear, as a wholesale business, in 1943; in 1959, I founded the Sydney Company as the sales arm of my previous company as well as the sales representative of other children's wear manufacturing companies. I'm sure that I had had the idea for the new company before going on my first safari, but plans for putting it into effect didn't take their final form until I returned. It was as if Africa represented a hiatus from business for me and left me with a feeling of wanting to surge forward when I came home. Maybe it was a continuation of the impulse of the kill or a carry-over of having stalked prey, but all my African safaris tended to push me into building up my business with greater energy.

Once the new business was under way and I was lucky enough to have good people to leave it to, I left for my second safari in 1960–1961.

It's romantic for most of us to think that the first time we fall in love or make love, it's the best. With time, we learn that experience can only improve love or love-making, and so it was with my going on safari. I can't honestly say my first one was the best. It gave me a great introduction to Africa, and it gave me the comfort of travelling with a friend to talk to and the security of knowing we could be links to the outside world in case one of us got sick or hurt. I had that kind of companionship on one other safari out of the ten that I took, when my son-in-law, Joel Halpern, came with me.

But my other safaris were probably better from the standpoint of adventure. Certainly my second safari, taken about eighteen months after my first one, was rewarding to me for three important reasons: I began to learn more about the people of Kenya—the white colonials and the Masai; I became a good friend of Robert Ruark, a newspaper writer and hunter who had become an African expert with his novel *Something of Value*; and in killing my first elephant, I began to learn more about the expectations and challenges I set for myself as a hunter.

I didn't intend to take my first elephant, although my hunting license allowed me to. Usually, you applied for a license to hunt a wide variety of game just to cover yourself. It meant taking a calculated risk, since you often didn't get back the cost of the license if you didn't take the animal. Sometimes this could really add up.

For instance, the fee for taking my first lion was about $150; toward the end of my safari days in 1980, the fee had gone up to $2,000. Sports hunters may grumble about this, but they really know it's for the good of the sport: licensing fees are used to protect hunting areas from poaching violations, so in a way they help insure that there will be game left to hunt.

But this particular elephant literally crossed my path and I had no choice but to kill him, according to the rules of good sportsmanship that I tried to follow.

My hunter, Bill Morley, our Wakamba gun-bearers and porters, and all the rest of our African staff were in southwest Kenya. We had made camp less than a mile from where a river and a narrow stream came together in a "V" shape. The morning after our first night there, it was evident that an elephant had moved through camp while we were asleep and not too early in the night either since his droppings were still quite warm! This happened for a few nights—the elephant never harmed our tents and never woke anyone either, but it was apparent we were in the path of him and his leafy food supply.

Without telling me or Bill, our camp boys decided to kill the elephant for his tusks. They probably could have gotten more money for the tusks, if they were a good pair, than they would have by working on safaris for a year.

Their plan called for them to stay up during the night and shoot a poisoned dart into the elephant. Many were from the Wakamba tribe, which had a reputation for being good elephant-hunters and they must have observed that this was a lone elephant, a bachelor who was in the habit of crossing back and forth over the stream every day and walking over the land we had camped on. They figured that with the poison in him, he'd only be able to travel about one-quarter of a mile before falling and that he'd never be able to ford the stream in his weakened condition.

Their object would be to wait until we left camp at about 5:00 A.M. to start the day's safari, and then they'd approach the sick animal and finish him off while we were still in the bush. They'd hack the tusks out and hide them until some future date after the safari had ended when they'd come back for them.

The first part of the plan—shooting the poison dart—worked, but the rest didn't because when morning came, we unexpectedly decided to break camp and move. Of course, this frustrated their attempt to retrieve the ivory from the wounded elephant and one of the gun-bearers who was on close terms with Bill told him what they had done. This was a huge offense on the part of the natives, but because of the close relationship between the hunter and his safari team, we decided not to turn the perpetrators over to the government police.

But we had a wounded, dying animal on our hands, and it was our moral obligation to finish the animal off. So Bill and I and about five or six blacks set off, found the animal lying on its side and breathing heavily, about one-half a mile from camp, and I put a bullet through his brain.

I felt no exaltation doing it, nor any great sorrow. It was more like a mercy killing; I was merely putting an animal that was going to die anyway out of its misery. That's part of a sports hunter's code of ethics—not to leave a wounded animal to die in pain in the bush. That feeling was in sharp contrast to the deep emotion I felt many years later in Rhodesia when I killed another elephant.

In that case, I had been on its spoor and stalked it on foot for miles. I personally think that stalking on foot is the true test of a hunter because it adds a kind of one-on-one dimension. When you and your prey are each on foot, you both have an advantage—you may have a gun, but the animal knows the area. I've had some real close calls hunting this way, but I think it's a good indication of your guts.

Anyway, I shot that elephant in Rhodesia when he was only about twenty-seven feet away from me. I used a .450 Magnum, which is like a cannon. The elephant had turned and was charging me with his ears way out and his trunk up in the air in an agitated manner as if he were using it like radar to feel where I was. I could see the spot directly through his ear where the bullet has its best chance of entering the brain and quickly killing him, and that's what I aimed for and got. The beast fell on his knees, gave me what seemed like a look of intense hatred, collapsed and died, and I broke down and cried, having seen this magnificent beast fall in front of me. It was a release of great emotion.

I felt a sense of exhilaration with this second elephant that I didn't get with my first. In that early case, I felt that the black crew members had really killed it—not me—even though I had put in the finishing shot. By poisoning it with a dart, they were really responsible for its death. I just speeded up the process.

There are some professional hunters, said a friend who was one, who believe that somehow it doesn't seem bad to kill something that you want very badly and have hunted very hard after. After all, life in Africa is all based on death—big predators killing weaker ones and then being killed themselves and the hyenas and vultures and ants finishing off the remains.

I don't know if I agree with all of that, but I do know I felt no real satisfaction after killing the first elephant—it was like doing my duty—but I had worked hard to bag my second elephant. It meant a constant alertness on my part during the stalk, and getting him did make me feel both intense joy and sorrow. That, by the way, was also the last elephant I shot—not out of lack of opportunity but by deliberate choice not to take another elephant trophy.

Two of the most amazing things happened after that first elephant died. As soon as the skinners had cut open the elephant's stomach, which is the normal procedure, and began hacking the tusks out from the skull, some Masai swarmed out of the bush and mounted the back of the elephant. They began stripping the thick, yellow fat from between the meat and the skin and anointed themselves with the fat; in some cases, they even devoured it. Obviously, fat, which is a part of their dietary needs, wasn't normally obtained from an elephant! The smell of the dead animal wasn't too bad, but the flies soon came and it became almost intolerable to stand by.

But the strangest part came next when a few Pygmies, whom we didn't even know were in the area, started to come timidly out of the bush and began taking away the insides of the animal that were lying next to it—the lungs, the heart, the intestines, and whatever other innards they were able to pull away. A few even reached into the belly to get to the entrails.

While this was going on, the skinners and the rest of our men were hacking the ivory from out of the creature's skull. To this day, I have no idea what happened to the tusks because I didn't want them. They were irregular and had no value to me, so I gave them to the men and whether they were ground up or cut into trinkets, I don't know. I do know though that after this the men were ready to kill for me.

Now normally this is not what happens when you shoot for the pot or for a trophy. Usually, after an animal is taken, the camp hands or skinners will move in and slit open the belly to let out any escaping gases. It has to be done quickly because otherwise the animal gets bloated with gas, which then gets into the skin and makes the hide unworthy of being preserved. Naturally, when an animal is shot and dies, his bowels also break open; he usually urinates as well and the whole thing really stinks. After a while you get used to it, and I didn't even notice it.

Once the animal is slit open, the skinners then cut it up as well as any surgeon or butcher might. They clean out any fat that may lie under the skin and put an enormous amount of salt on it, which helps preserve it, especially in the hot areas we were moving in. They've also got to get into the belly and pull out the viscera—the heart, lungs, intestines, and everything. It usually comes out in one piece. I once tried doing this with a zebra, but frankly I was happier letting the skinners do their job.

Among African tribes, I later found out, the heart of the animal would usually be given to the hunter who killed it to eat. The heart means life, and it's quite an honor to get it. On safari, I'd usually turn it over to the professional hunter, who'd turn it over to one of the African headmen who came with us.

Since we travelled with twenty-five or thirty men, we did shoot for the pot. Although some men didn't eat any meat, most of them did. We ate plains game—grass-eaters like antelope, gazelle, and zebra—and the hunters and I would usually get the cut along the back, called the brisket or the filet. It usually had a fatty, burnt taste like a cross between beef and lamb. The blacks would eat the meat on the legs and forelegs. I had tried elephant meat, but I never ate carnivores like lion or leopard.

Watching the way the Masai and the Pygmies behaved with that first elephant certainly amazed me, but even on my first safari, I had started being interested in how differently the Africans lived. Whenever my wife, Edna, and I had travelled to Europe, Cuba, South and Central America, we always went to the native marketplace where the people shopped and sometimes even to the red-light districts where they drank and danced. That's because I'm always on the lookout for anything that smacks of real life. It's part of being always alert to things around me, which is a natural part of my personality. If I stay at the hotels like the Plaza in New York, the George V in Paris, or any of the fine hotels in the world, which I've done lots of times, I get luxury treatment, but it's not a real slice of life and that's what I want to experience.

So in Nairobi also, I sought out the native market on my very first trip because that would give me an idea of the foods the natives ate, the clothes they wore, and how they lived in contrast to what I'd see staying in the so-called civilized part of the city. Nairobi was, even in 1958, an unusually large, modern city—the only one of the its kind between Cairo to the north and Salisbury, Rhodesia, to the south.

In the city's big hotels, the black natives wore red fezzes and bleached white shirts, but their faces were impassive and you couldn't get any sense of what they were really like. But in the native quarter, things were different.

What I saw and smelled in the Nariobi marketplace was lots of food I didn't recognize and some I did; almost everywhere flies were crawling over mangoes, yams, and melons, and goats' and sheeps' heads.

I saw a lot of citified tribespeople—the men wearing drab, cast-off, army-issue clothes or ragged-looking, second-hand shirts and shorts while the women were in shapeless but brightly colored dresses. Even though they wore Western-style clothing, they didn't seem that comfortable with Western ways: at one stall, I watched some men haunched down on their knees, eating some food with their fingers. Finding someone who spoke a kind of pidgin-English, I asked if they ever used forks or spoons and the man answered that those were for white people to eat with and weren't comfortable for them to use.

There was also the native color you'd expect in an East African marketplace: a few Kikuyu men still wore cork-sized ear plugs; some Nandi and Wakama men still stretched their earlobes and tucked the pierced bottoms neatly over the tops; and goatskin-caped Masai with ocher-colored clay painted on their skins and hair would swagger by carrying lethal-looking spears. Then there were Indian merchants—the men wearing turbans, the women in saris with red dots daubed in the center of their foreheads, and Arab traders in caftans and burnooses.

Later in the bush on the first safari, I also began to pick up on tribal differences. It became apparent in camp that you couldn't lump all Africans together when I noticed there'd be four or five cook-fires going at the same time in addition to the one where our food was being prepared. That was because different tribes ate different foods and didn't even mix much socially. Most of the time, they didn't even speak the same language and you'd have three, four, or five different tongues going, which is why you needed a good hunter—he'd be able to speak some of the languages and if he didn't, he'd have a trusted headman from the different groups who'd do the translating.

I never learned any native languages, but I was told that in the downtown Nairobi market, you could hear dozens of dialects—Swahili, Meru, Embu, Wakamba, Kipsigi, Kavirondo, Masai, Somali, and Nandi, for example.

The African tribes, I also heard, were known for different things in Kenya: the Wakamba and the Turkana were supposed to be the best elephant hunters; the Masai were lion hunters, while the Kikuyu were known for tending herds and raising crops. When I was first there in 1958, the Kikuyu were also known for making up the bulk of the Mau Mau uprising—a native terrorist group that wanted to eliminate British control over Kenya. We were lucky not to be bothered by them when we were in the bush, but my friend Gerry and I were told not to walk around unarmed at night in downtown Nairobi on our way to places like the Equator Club or to a restaurant.

During these first two safaris, I was a careful and distant observer of the natives until something happened on the second safari that got me interested in studying the Masai habits more closely.

My hunter, Bill Morley, and I were camping near Masai Mara, the native reserve, when we came across a group of Masai on the move. Now, the Masai are nomads who follow their cattle. As soon as one area gets over-grazed, they leave their homes or "manyattas," which are built of twigs and kept together by cow dung. They move closer to new pasture land where they build new manyattas.

This particular group, I happened to see, was led by one man, probably the chieftain. Other men followed him; then came women, children, and finally the elderly and sick people who straggled along behind. At the very end was one old man who limped along with a staff. He did his best to keep up, but the space between him and the group got bigger when suddenly about ten or twelve wild dogs came out of the bush and started circling around him, yapping, and nipping in and out around his feet. These grayish-brown dingoes are about the size of a large-sized terrier, and despite their size, they can be vicious killers when they hunt in packs. The old man took a few swings at them with his staff, but they were tenacious and just hung in there.

I was about a hundred to a hundred and forty yards away and was amazed that he didn't call out to anyone. Not one single person in the group ahead ever turned around to look at him, much less to protect him. I just couldn't stand by and do nothing while the dogs tried to grab him, so I fired off some shots and got a few of them with my shotgun, but not all. The man looked surprised and stopped swinging, but I could tell from his face that he was in pain and expected to die.

I would have thought that the gunshots would have caused some of the people ahead to come back and help the man, but no one came and the dogs finally knocked him down and tore him apart in about three or four minutes.

I remember shouting at my hunter, "For God's sake, are you going to let this thing happen?"

He just said, "Sydney, it's a part of their way of life."

When it was over, our boys moved in and cut off the dingoes' tails to turn in for bounty money. Somehow that disgusted me almost as much as the man's death. The game wardens apparently disapproved of the dingoes' method of killing and had a policy of shooting them on sight and rewarding anyone else who did.

I found out later from my hunter that when the Masai leave one area for a new one, they never turn around. Those who are strong enough to follow do so, but those who can't keep up and fall behind are left to the predators—the wild dogs, the leopards, and even the hyenas. Nor, on a trek, would the group stop to bury them—they'd be left for the vultures.

The whole scene was so alien to me—the ugliness of the man's death and what I took to be indifference on the part of the Masai—that I decided to try to get closer to the tribe on another trip to learn more about their social habits.

Meantime, my hunter's behavior had also given me something to think about. He seemed to accept the Masai behavior for what it was rather than judging it, the way my inclination had been.

The professional hunters themselves seemed to be a peculiar group, and the ones I came to know led lives that I found damned attractive. I never felt I wanted to be one of them, but at the same time, I enjoyed being with them—it was like being invited to play with the big boys.

Most of the hunters seem to epitomize a free-wheeling life-style. They had tremendous freedom of movement, which I found appealing. If they were married, their wives stayed home and minded their farm along with the children while the men seemed to come and go, depending on when they had booked a hunt with clients. If they weren't married, they worked as farm managers when they weren't off hunting. They were young, in physically great shape, and they were basically renegades. When they weren't on safari, the single ones were bums, womanizers, and beer-drinkers, but in a harmless way.

I never met one who looked as if he were rich, but it didn't matter. In a way, they were men who were allowed to be boys—they didn't hold a 9:00 A.M.-5:00 P.M. job, and they didn't worry about foreclosure if the crops didn't come in. They were just interested in the good hunt—the largest lion, the heaviest Kudu horn, or whatever.

In contrast, there was me—traditional, respectable, a hard-working businessman and a caring husband and father. None of them probably ever owned a suit while back home I had a closet full of them. When I went on safari, I kept those business and dress suits at home and put on what I call my "Boy Scout clothes." Those old khaki hunting clothes represented freedom and a kind of scary fun. Sometimes, like when I tried to help the old Masai man with the dogs, wearing that "Boy Scout" suit also meant doing good deeds, but that wasn't my primary intention in putting it on—I wore it for fun.

The hunters and I did share one thing in common: we all survived by being alert to our environment, whether it was the bush or business trends, and we lived by our wits or following our educated instincts. These qualities were probably what made me enjoy hunting for trophies—animals that met certain, exact specifications like judging pets or plants in a ribboned show.

Hunting for trophies meant you had to be a patient, discriminating stalker—you carefully choose your victim, if you want to call it that, to represent the best of its species—and then you went after him. If I was going after a greater Kudu with a triple curve in its horns, for example, I might pass one by at 6:00 A.M. because I felt I'd come across a better specimen later in the day—an animal with better placed horns or ones that were more symmetrical or shapelier. Also, unless it was a matter of protecting myself or someone else, I'd never take a female. Females just aren't trophy material, except for zebras where there's no difference between males and females that can be observed.

Sometimes the sport of stalking the animal's spoor—of tracking its footprints or droppings—became even more exciting than the so-called moment of truth or the kill. Many a time I bent down to feel a ball of crap to see from its age how far or how long ago the animal had passed by.

This kind of hunting wasn't shared by lots of tourists to Africa in those days. Most of them came on once-in-a-lifetime trips to grab as much game as their licenses would allow. Then, since this was before customs regulations went into effect, if they weren't completely satisfied with the set of elephant tusks they had taken, they could always march into a shop in Nairobi and buy another pair. For ninety percent of them, having hunted in Africa was just an ego trip. For me, it was a way of life that under different times and circumstances I might have enjoyed living.

One of the men in Kenya who understood my

passion for trophy-hunting was Robert Ruark. Although he wasn't a professional hunter, he was a great sports hunter as well as being a *New York Times* correspondent. He had also written the 1955 bestseller about Kenya, *Something of Value*. I met him by chance when we were both staying at the Norfolk Hotel.

The Norfolk had something of a legendary reputation in Nairobi. President Teddy Roosevelt had set off on safari from here in 1909; General Baden-Powell, founder of the Boy Scouts, had been a guest; and in the 1960s, it also became a favorite of Ernest Hemingway. It was unpretentious and comfortable in the way that old British hunting lodges or country homes were furnished. With a front facade that resembled a Tudor-style building, the most notable feature about the hotel was its cottages out back. They were built around a cobbled courtyard on sixteen-foot-high stilts to allow any stray animals to wander beneath them.

I had just checked into the hotel and had gotten into bed around 10:00 P.M. Sometime around midnight my sleep was disturbed by a loud ruckus that came from the cottage opposite mine. Upon opening my door, I looked out and saw a man at the top of steps of the cottage, reeling from side to side and looking as if he were going to topple over. He was obviously very drunk and "balls naked," as the expression goes. But the noise came from someone dressed in a Muslim gown, who just as obviously had been pushed down the flight of stairs where he was now lying. Luckily, he wasn't hurt because as soon as I opened my door, he scurried away.

I ran down the steps of my cottage up to where the drunken man was standing, turned him around, marched him inside, put him in bed, and then left, closing the door behind me.

The next day I spent around town getting ready to leave for safari at 4:00 A.M. the next morning. When I got back to the hotel in the afternoon, I found a note pinned to my bed, which said, "Please join me for a drink, R.R." Not knowing who R.R. was, I inquired at the reception desk and was told that it was Mr. Robert Ruark, African correspondent for the *New York Times* and other syndicated newspapers.

I met with Ruark on the veranda where he had a bottle of Scotch on the table and quite a few drinks under his belt already. I introduced myself to him, and he asked me to sit down and thanked me for helping him the night before. He had gotten that information from one of the hotel employees who must have figured out what I done based on Ruark's past need for assistance.

Ruark was so full of interesting stories about Africa that we spoke and drank without eating from the time I met him at about 5:00 P.M. to about 2:00 A.M. the next morning. It was the first, but not the last time, that I found myself tossing drinks into nearby plants or shrubbery whenever he turned away or got up to urinate because there was no way I could keep up with his drinking. Nor did I want to. I wanted him to go on speaking so I could learn everything I could from him about Africa, and I figured the only way I could do that was by letting him drink and talk while I stayed fairly sober.

Ruark was fascinating to me because he not only knew all about Africa, but he knew all about Africans. He had a journalist's knack for getting the inside story and knew all the Happy Valley gossip—those were wealthy British settlers who had vast farms and coffee plantations outside of Nairobi. You could see them congregating on the veranda or in the bar when they came to town—chic women dressed in summer dresses and nylons and men with burly sun-tanned legs showing under shorts. Between the drinking and bed-hopping they did, Ruark described it as living the fast life in a slow country.

He also knew what was happening with the Mau Maus and the political unrest at the time. The Mau Maus were terrorists, drawn mainly from the Kikuyu tribe, who invaded farms, setting them on fire and attacking the white settlers. They were just as brutal to their fellow Africans who didn't join them—dismembering them and impaling their bodies on poles. The danger was greatest out in isolated farms in the country, but even in the city there was unease at night and white men always carried sidearms for protection.

Ruark was on a first-name basis with two Kikuyu leaders who eventually became important political figures: Jomo Kenyatta, the first elected president of Kenya, and Tom Mboya, his main adviser. I had met both men earlier on a previous safari and enjoyed having my opinions of them confirmed by Ruark.

Our meeting had taken place in a prison. Along with my hunter and a bush pilot, I had flown to an area to scout out hunting possibilities. There was a kind of makeshift prison nearby where the British had impounded thousands of Mau Maus. The stockade was nothing more than a fence of bamboo poles stuck in the ground about eight-to-ten-inches apart. It was being used as some kind of temporary holding camp, but apparently it was quite safe even though it was guarded by just a handful of British soldiers. At any

Leopard taken on one of earlier safaris in Kenya

East Africa, lush Rift Valley in background

Rarely has any hunter been successful in taking two greater kudus at the same time

New Zealand, South Island, Mount Cook in background

Zebra, Zululand, South Africa

Peda-cycling in Thailand, Far East Asia

With Guatemalan Indian children when monitoring their living conditions, Central America

Trophy giraffe, South Africa's Transvaal bordering on Botswana

Joining in native dance in Albania

Tribal female entering thatched hut near Victoria Falls, Zambia

Cattle auction with son-in-law (Rhodesia, later called Zimbabwe)

Part of family at the Jarkows' Long Island home

time, the blacks could have parted the poles and left the camp, but perhaps because they were well-fed and treated, there was no attempt to escape.

When our plane landed, a group of about twenty prisoners came out to greet us out of curiosity. One of the headmen who spoke English, as did many of the others, was a huge, black man with a full head of white hair. He was Jomo Kenyatta. Directly behind him, and always near him, was Tom Mboya—a young man with a dynamic personality who impressed me as being very smart. I thought later that he was probably the brains behind the entire independence movement in Kenya.

We spent some time together talking, and then my group took off. Over the next few years, I also met them a few times more with Ruark in Nairobi. It wasn't until these men became leaders of the country that I realized the importance of my meeting them. More than twenty years later, as a representative of the Anti-Defamation League, I'd meet another group of government leaders in Nairobi to thank them for allowing Israeli pilots to refuel their airplanes before making the raid on Entebbe, Uganda.

But that was a long time off in the future. Ruark respected Kenyatta and Mboya as individuals, but he had reservations about Kenya without the British in control. Like many whites who came out to Kenya when it was part of the British Empire, he had a fairly arrogant attitude toward blacks, which he kept even after the country became an independent nation in 1963. According to him, the mark of a successful black African bureaucrat was to have a white mistress, usually from France or Belgium. Other African old-hands were more tolerant about change: even in 1966, my old friend and hunter, Bill Jenvey, wrote me, saying,

"It's possible that your press may carry sensational news of political unrest here. There is some but nothing to worry about—Africa will be like this for the next hundred years."

Ruark and I kept up our friendship over the years, and Edna and I visited him at his home in Malaga, Spain. The chemistry was just right between us, although in his case the chemistry was probably mixed with an awful lot of booze.

In a way, hanging out with Ruark was a little like being friendly with the hunters, since they all led a wilder life than I normally did. Spending time with them and hearing their stories was my way, I guess, of flirting with that kind of life. I remember Ruark once tried to tempt me into stopping over in Italy with him on my way home. He knew all sorts of film people there and I'd have no trouble finding a young girl to go home with, he said. But I figured this was nothing for me to fool around with—besides, I already had what I wanted waiting at my home for me.

Of course, what we also had in common was a love of adventure. I was never unaware of the chance of danger in Africa and I was always alert to it as a real possibility, but I rarely consciously felt physically unsafe in Africa although there were probably dozens of times when I could have been killed—when I went crocodile-hunting at night, when a lion stalked me, or even when I went to put on my shoes in the morning and always had to check to make sure there was no scorpion waiting inside one, ready to sting me.

There were lots of times when the adrenaline was pumped up and I sweated bullets, but I'm basically an optimist. Part of my mental make-up is not to dwell on negative thoughts like fear. With the exception of being afraid of anyone in my family getting sick, I honestly don't think I have any physical or mental fears. Being in Africa was always a kind of expanding experience for me—I kept challenging myself there and meeting my goals. If I had had any real fears, I wouldn't have been able to keep doing that for over twenty-two years!

Chapter Five
Stalking Big Prey

Most sports hunters in Africa go after the Big Five trophies: the elephant, the buffalo, the lion, the leopard, and the rhino. Whether it's because of their bulk or their ferocity, these are the traditional manly prizes.

But, in my opinion, the real trophies are the beautiful exotic game, whether they're found in the mountains like the nyala or on the plains like the black sable, the greater kudu, or the Grant's gazelle. I look at them as art or sculpture, with the right amount of curves, swirls, arcs, turns, length, and balance to the horn. To me, it's almost the same as admiring and having a Renoir.

On the other hand, the only place you'll probably find a perfect specimen of a black-maned, tawny lion is the zoo. In the bush, a lion's skin is constantly being torn by briars and branches while the sun bleaches its hair, so if you want an aesthetically undamaged specimen, you'll have to look a long time. As for the rhino—white or black—I've never wanted to go after one. I certainly never had any use for ground-up rhino horn as an aphrodisiac, and I can't imagine mounting a rhino head as a trophy. I feel the same way about the looks of the cantankerous hippo, which is why I've never tried to bag one of them either. In a sense, I guess, I've been as much a collector of beautiful skins and trophies as I've been a hunter.

But I do respect most all animals—the leopard, lion, buffalo, and elephant, especially because they're such fearsome adversaries. Those are the animals that would just as soon take you, so you try to take them instead. That's why when you approach a lion, you hope that the animal has just been feeding.

In the case of the lion I went after in the Kalahari Desert in 1973, I wasn't at all sure if the lion was hungry or not. Neither was I always certain who was stalking whom, since at one point the lion circled around and seemed to be stalking me and my hunter.

But I should have known this wasn't a usual lion hunt from an omen I got from another animal on this safari—a big boa constrictor that tried snuggling against me for warmth in the middle of the night.

Because I was hunting lion for a trophy, I had made a special point to consider the size and quality of the animal. Lions that live in heavily forested areas are likely to have their skins torn and scarred by heavy thorns and sharp tree limbs, so I decided to hunt for one either on the open savannah or the desert.

That's why the autumn of 1973 found me on the hard-packed sand of Botswana's Kalahari Desert. Clumps of scraggly grass and some bushes acted as cover for the lions, yet there was little there to damage the lion's skin. Despite what most people think about deserts, the northeastern part of the Kalahari has enough waterholes and oases to attract plains game like zebra, gemsbok, and springbok; their presence, in turn, attracts the lion. Even when conditions are really dry, I understand, these desert antelope get moisture from the plants and juicy roots they eat while predators like the lion survive on the body fluids of their victims.

I was with Ronnie Blackbeard, who was all of

twenty-three years old; at that time, he was the only professional hunter born in Botswana, although at the time of his birth it was called the Bechuanaland Protectorate.

Early one morning, Ronnie and I set out from our fly camp—a temporary camp of lightweight fly tents you use when you're on the move—and came upon evidence of a lone male. Judging from its droppings and the size of its paw prints (about eight inches across), the animal was probably a young bachelor, maybe weighing about four hundred pounds.

We followed the spoor until 5:00 P.M., when we went back to camp. The next day we took sleeping bags with us in case we had to track the animal throughout the night. By late afternoon, it became obvious that we were moving in on the lion. But he also had picked up our scent and from his footprints, which were behind us, it was equally apparent that he was stalking us.

It's a funny thing about the openness of the desert. Normally when you look out on landscape, the land and sky come together at the horizon. But on the desert, the earth never seems to meet the sky. Probably that has to do with the heat vapors rising up from the ground and blocking the horizon. But that openness, together with the desert's tall grass, gives you and the lion a similar degree of cover or exposure to each other. You, of course, have the advantage of field glasses or rifle scopes, but the lion has an edge with his sense of smell and knowledge of the area.

At any rate, we decided to let our native trackers, skinners, and bearers go back to camp and that we'd sleep out.

As dusk fell, we set up a fire for camping. We needed the fire, first, to keep the lion or any other animal away, and second, because in the Kalahari it was common for the temperature to drop from 110 degrees during the day to 30 or 40 degrees at night.

We positioned our sleeping bags pointing away from the fire; I was about three-to-five feet away from it, and Ronnie was about the same distance behind me. Soon after the stars came out, it got so cold that we crawled into our sleeping bags and pulled the zippers up almost over our heads. In fact, I think I fell asleep wearing a hat to keep my head warm.

The next thing I knew I felt something nudging my back in the middle of the night. I couldn't imagine what it was, so I turned my head, peeked out of the bag, and called over quietly to Ronnie because my first thought was that he was alerting me that the lion was close by. He was asleep but as soon as he heard me, he unzipped his bag in seconds and told me to roll over toward the fire. When your professional hunter tells you to do something, you do it, so in a flash I pulled down my sleeping bag zipper too. As I rolled away from the object behind me, the moonlight revealed a huge snake, possibly a boa constrictor, which had probably been seeking some warmth and had found a nice spot to nestle against my sleeping bag. That snake was so fast that within seconds he must have covered fifty yards or more and moved off into the dark.

Neither Ronnie nor I had any inclination to go after the snake, and I know I slept fretfully for the rest of the night. Finally, we got up when it was still pitch black and got ready to track the lion again.

It took most of the day until about 4:00 P.M., when we came to an area filled with huge anthills, some of which were eight to ten feet high and four to five feet wide at the base. The lion, by now, was as aware of us as we were of him and sometimes no more than thirty to forty yards separated us. We kept circling around those anthills, trying to get into a position where a killing shot could be made. The animal was so close to us that if I didn't put him away with the first shot, I'd have a wounded lion on my hands who was a hell of a lot stronger than I was.

All of a sudden, and completely unnoticed until now, we saw, at about two hundred yards off, a female lion who had probably lost her mate and was intent upon establishing a relationship with the male we were hunting. So there we were, Ronnie and I and the lions, circling in and out of the anthills, trying to put ourselves in position for the moment of truth.

Finally, as the male came out of the shadow of a large anthill, he quartered on me so that I was able to make a very telling shot at his right fore-shoulder, thus breaking his ability to charge us. The animal hit the ground with an enormous roar, and I immediately pumped another shot from my .375 gauge rifle into him when I simultaneously heard a scream from my hunter who was backing me up to "DROP." Instinctively, I hit the ground and just as I did, I felt the hot wind and smell of the female lion, who had come at me from the side and behind. The animal was so close to me on its leap that when I turned my head from the ground toward her, I could actually see the fangs and outspread paws.

Because it was late in the day, we had to skin the lion before the sun went down. Otherwise, if we came back for it the next day, both the heat of the sun and scavengers like vultures, hyenas, and jackals would get to it and ruin the skin. So, there we were: the female lion pacing back and forth in the distance, me sweating bullets as I stood guard with my rifle and watched the lioness, and Ronnie skinning the lion. Fortunately, because of the looseness of their body skins, lions are skinned rather easily by slitting them from belly to crotch. It seemed like an eternity, but from bullet shot until the skin came off, it probably only took forty minutes.

No sooner had we collected the skin and the head and set off back on foot to camp—and it was a heavy load of about 150–200 pounds—than the female moved in to eat from the rest of the carcass. Pretty ironic when you think that she had probably tried to bond with the male lion because she was either in heat or had lost her mate. But that's the law of the jungle. The strong will prey on the weak, the sick, the dying, and the dead.

Another badge of a hunter's successful safari is bagging a leopard, partly because the hunting procedures used are quite elaborate. In my case, the leopard was especially rewarding because we had been asked to kill it by some villagers whom it had been terrorizing. The year, as I recall, was 1969–1970 and we were hunting in East Africa—an area of Kenya next to Tanzania. As on most safaris, we traded with natives for things like maize, fresh fruit, or vegetables, and at one community the people complained that a leopard was marauding their small herds and destroying their gardens. They asked us to try to kill the animal, so we decided to stay and see if we could take it.

Now, unlike hunting lion, you don't go out and just stalk the leopard. You set a kind of trap for it, called a blind. First, you have to get bait—a freshly killed animal of 300–400 pounds usually does it, so I got a wildebeest. The wildebeest is the stupidest-looking of all antelopes—grotesque, ridiculously bearded, and high-humped like a bison, with a tail that's always wagging in a foolish way. Really, I think the wildebeest is fit only for crossword puzzles under the three-letter word *gnu.*

My hunter and I cut the wildebeest's belly open so that the odor of the entrails would attract the leopard. Then we laid down more scent in the area by tying the bait to the rear bumper of our Land Rover and making a huge circle about half-a-mile wide. We kept circling and trailing the animal behind us, bringing it closer to the point we wanted it. Next, we selected a tree, hoisted the wildebeest up eight-to-ten feet above the ground, and tied it to a branch. Finally, we set up a blind of twigs and leaves about fifty yards away and covered it up so that it looked like part of the natural features of the land. A small space was left open for our gunsights.

Because the leopard is a nocturnal animal, we would get to the blind at about 2:00 A.M. and wait for the sunrise. The theory was that when the sun rose in the east, it would cast its light onto the tree where the bait was and that way we'd be able to see and shoot the leopard. During those hours that we waited in the small blind, we had to be very careful not to move or make any sound because the leopard is extremely sensitive to noise. We couldn't talk, sneeze, or even clear our throats. If we had to communicate with each other, we did it by hand signals.

But just as bad for us, we also had to watch out for any unnatural odors because the leopard also has a very sharp sense of smell. We couldn't use insect repellent, for instance, to protect us from insects, much less pass wind or go to the bathroom, because the odor would be strong enough to warn off the leopard. It was like lying in suspended animation for four hours usually lying down on my stomach with the gun propped up in front of me or across my knees if I was sitting up. The hunter was about three yards behind me for back-up. We knew damn well we better not fall asleep or we might miss our chance!

It took a great degree of concentration and stamina to stay in that blind, as well as a helluva desire to kill the animal. Sometimes you'd get so mad, you'd wish the sun would come up with or without the animal appearing just so you could go back to camp and get some sleep.

We spent four days, or nights really, in that blind without firing a single shot before deciding we'd give it one more night and then quit. That fifth night passed quietly, with both me and my hunter lying belly down in the soil. Then, as the sun started to come up, my hunter tapped my foot and motioned to me that he saw some movement in the baited tree ahead of us. After figuring out what his gestures meant and looking through my gunsight, I finally saw a reflection of sun on the animal's eye. Just the white of his eye literally betraying the leopard's presence!

It was an incredible moment and after all this time, I was really anxious to get off a shot. I knew that leopards generally feed from above the kill with their heads down, so I decided to guess where the heart was and aim for that rather than shooting at the head and ruining it as a trophy. But as soon as I took the shot, I could tell from the "plunk" of the bullet against the animal that it was a belly shot. This meant I would have a sick and mean animal on my hands.

No sooner was the hit made than the animal leaped to the ground without uttering a sound and ran off into the forest. Any animal that's shot or sick will instinctively seek some protective cover, so it was natural for this leopard to run off into the thick forest that was around us. But the creed of every true sportsman is that a wounded animal has to be pursued until he's killed. It's not a code of honor that's written down, but you just know that no matter how tired you are, how edgy you feel, you have to go off after the animal or else you'll lose all respect for yourself and the respect of your black crew as well.

With me leading into the heavily wooded area, we followed the animal's blood spoor. Even though the sun was climbing in the sky over the canopy of forest, underneath the hardwood trees, it was still dark and cool. The air was moist with humidity because this was a tropical forest, but at least it was cool and that was a plus because the heat would have been stifling under all that pressure. Because the area was so thick with trees, vines, and tall grasses, my hunter and I had switched from rifles to shotguns. In close quarters like this, the spray of a shotgun had a better chance of stopping the beast than a rifle shot, which might not hit a vital organ.

For almost three hours, we followed the leopard, even though he was able to move through the trees as well as on the ground. At times we were only fifteen feet away from each other. But the area was so overgrown that I was unable to get the gun in a position to get off a shot. The leopard, meantime, who was threatened by us, was still moving around and at times actually stalked us with the intent of rushing us.

Finally, I got close enough and clear enough to get off a shot. Since the leopard was facing my way and getting ready to leap at me, I did the only thing I could.

I shot him straight in the face. The shotgun blast just about tore its head off.

At this point, through their own unique communication system, the natives found out that the animal was killed. About twenty or thirty of them came into the forest and tied the leopard's forelegs and back legs to a long tree limb and carried it back to their village. I was exhausted, physically and emotionally, and could only think of getting back to camp. I came out of the bush with my clothes all torn from the brambles and thorns. When you're stalking your prey as intently as we had been, you have no time to notice any physical discomfort like scratches and tears, but it had been so rough that even my leather boots were destroyed.

No sooner did I come out into their clearing than I could hear the sounds of a celebration the villagers had spontaneously put together. They mounted me on two long tree branches held together with a seat in the middle and carried me around for an hour, singing and dancing around their fire. I held up as long as I could, but I was so dead tired that after an hour I had to beg them to stop the celebration. I lay down in a tent that had been set up for me, and the next thing I knew I had slept for twenty-four hours and lost about twelve pounds.

Quite a strange and exhilarating experience for a boy from Brooklyn!

Safaris like that did put my life into perspective, although truthfully when I was in Africa I didn't think much about my life back home. It's only in looking back at those hunts that I see how unusual they were. First, the opportunities for going on safari became more and more limited during the 1970s as many of the new

African nations started putting restrictions on game-hunting. Licenses became more expensive, and there were fewer places where hunting was allowed. While tourists were still going out into the bush, they were armed with cameras and long-lenses, and not with heavy-gauge rifles.

I can also realize now how truly odd it must have seemed for someone like me to have kept on hunting game in Africa. One safari, sure. But two, three, four, five, and more was a bit excessive, I suppose. When most middle-aged men like myself were dodging traffic in Manhattan, there I was literally charging into a Cape buffalo herd with the intent of taking one down!

I took my buffalo in 1965 in northern Rhodesia, which was still under British control at the time and one of the few African countries still hospitable to hunters. The area we hunted in was mostly a high, rolling plateau of waving green or brown grasses, depending on the season. There were gentle hills and a moderate number of trees for cover. Of special interest to me, these high and central velds of Rhodesia were home to vast herds of Cape buffalo—fierce, black beasts weighing hundreds and even thousands of pounds, with massive, curved horns that measure nearly four to five feet across.

My hunter was Pookie Darlow, a huge, jolly man who was tough as hell on the outside, yet also a very talented artist with a delicate touch in his wildlife paintings. According to Pookie, we would need a special plan to hunt buffalo because of the way they grazed and moved. Buffalo are grass-eating herd animals; as many as five or six hundred will travel in an elliptical-shaped group. In order to get a trophy-sized buffalo, you have to first identify him and then break him out of the herd. The identifying part was easy: usually the outer circle of animals consists of the adolescent bulls; then as you move in you find younger males, females, and calves. At the very core of a herd this size, there will probably be eight to ten main bulls, weighing about two thousand pounds each, so there's a lot of beef on the hoof there.

But breaking the herd apart to get to one of the major bulls isn't so easy. Pookie's method was to make the buffalos think that our Land Rover was a threat to them—a strange-looking animal charging them. Our plan was to plow into the animals and to separate out a bull. At that point, I would jump out of the moving vehicle, find a position to keep an eye on the bull, and wait for Pookie to circle back so he could get out of the Rover and act as back-up while I tried to take the bull. Remember, both he and I felt strongly about shooting the buffalo on foot rather than from a moving car because we felt that way was the fairest kind of chase. We also felt we had to be at least two hundred feet away from any vehicle before stalking our game.

We spotted a good herd about five hundred yards away from us and positioned the Land Rover so we'd drive directly into this mass of animal flesh. There was Pookie at the wheel, beeping the car horn, me playing lookout by standing up in something like a turret, and two gun-bearers beating at the sides of the vehicle with large wooden sticks to make loud noises. We were all screaming at the tops of our voices to get the herd's attention.

Within seconds of starting to do this, the animals were alerted and looked at us in this glaring manner, a blank-looking stare. The herd broke and scattered in a thundering roar of hooves, and after spotting a promising-looking bull, I dropped over the side of the Rover and sprinted over to a nearby hill while Pookie and the others drove off.

It was important for me to do two things: to keep my gun cocked and to protect myself against any sudden turn and rush from the herd. The way to do that was to find a properly sized tree so that I could throw myself down on the ground and wrap my body around the trunk. Then, if a buffalo rushed me, I'd get a lot of his hot breath, and the shit scared out of me, but his curled horns wouldn't be able to gore me. Thank God, I never had the experience of those huge horns against my body.

I knew Pookie was supposed to circle around and return on foot with the two gun-bearers, but there was a delay in his coming back. But meantime, the herd had started to regroup. I had my eye on one huge bull and I didn't want to lose him, so I decided I'd go in and take him on my own. It was improper of me to do it without my hunter nearby, and damned unsafe too, but sometimes in situations like this, you act more on instinct than on conscious thought. Besides, my adrenaline was really running high from our noisy charge!

The bull I had picked out was looking at me from about forty yards away. He started snorting, pushing his feet back into the ground, and getting ready to charge. It's not that he saw me, really, since buffalo have very poor eyes, but he had picked up my scent and was turning and searching the air to sense where my scent was coming from. As soon as he turned his shoulder on me, I took careful aim with my .375 rifle—which is a lot of gun—and hit him in the heart.

The animal looked at me, snorted, and fell to the

ground. Apparently, the shot had broken his shoulder and that's why he fell forward on his forelegs. By instinct, the part of the herd that was standing nearby started to put distance between themselves and him. Equally by instinct, the buffalo struggled to get up, tried to assume a charging position, and came at me for a short distance. By this time, Pookie had come around and was standing behind me as back-up. I fired off another shot into the buffalo, but he was not going to die.

Instead, he veered around and started moving away from us at a slow trot. He struggled but he kept moving and at times he seemed to gain strength. He'd stop, turn around, eye us and paw the ground with his hooves as if he was getting ready to charge, and I'd put another shot into him. He'd stop, turn, limp off, and try to keep going. Even though I knew that the animal had a direct heart hit, which normally would have killed any other animal, this one just kept moving away from us. We followed him on foot for close to ten miles over nearly three hours.

Eventually, I put a total of eight shots into him before he died. When we opened him up, we found all eight shots were in his heart or an inch or two away from it. Even the first shot, which had penetrated his foreleg near the shoulder, had lodged in his heart. It's remarkable what a powerfully strong animal he was. It almost made Pookie forgive me for taking the foolish step of firing on a wild beast when I was totally alone. Then again, the idea of charging into a tightly packed buffalo herd in an open-side Land Rover also seems pretty foolish to me now.

But, by far, one of the stupidest hunts I ever went on—from the standpoint of putting myself in danger—

wasn't for a traditional big-game trophy. I didn't even come home with a skin, a head, a set of horns, or any other prize from this hunt aside from some really ballsy memories. It was the time I hunted crocodile at night on the Chobe River in Botswana in 1975.

More than any other hunt, this one took place in a dangerous environment with a minimum amount of back-up net—and that's why, looking back now, I think of it as stupid. As risky as hunting four-footed predators can be, you always have space to run and that can give you or your hunter enough time to get off a saving shot. Even when I hunted the short-tempered Cape buffalo, I knew I could find a tree to help protect myself. But when it's pitch black except for pairs of red eyes gleaming at you and you're belly-down in a narrow dugout feeling each ridge on the spine of a Nile crocodile bumping the keel beneath you, you truly have no place to hide and you better aim straight.

I was with Mike Cameron, a good-looking, well-built young man in his late twenties who had a reputation for being very popular with female clients. In fact, he was regarded as the most eligible bachelor in Victoria Falls. Of course, I couldn't help noticing that when I began going on safaris, many of the hunters and I were the same age, but as the years went by, more and more of them got younger. But I was sufficiently mature as a hunter at this time to work with a younger man, and I like to think it gave me an opportunity to show him something about hunting game and working with clients. I had just come out of hunting in the Kalahari Desert with Ronnie Blackbeard, another young hunter. Since we were up near the Chobe River in northern Botswana right near Victoria Falls, I had changed from white hunters to a river specialist.

As part of the ever-flowing Zambezi River system in a country that's otherwise mostly hot, harsh, and dry, the area around the Chobe is rich in wildlife. Some of Africa's last great free-roaming herds of zebras, sable antelopes, and elephants are found near here. The river is home to hippos, waxy white night-blooming water lilies, and to the Nile crocodile.

At lengths sometimes reaching twenty-four feet and weighing as much as a ton, these crocodiles are known for eating whatever and whomever they want to. One legend, or "fish story," I heard had one of these prehistoric water monsters making a meal out of a full-grown ox that had wandered too close to the river bank. Even experts agree the Nile crocodile is more ferocious and aggressive than its cousins—the American alligator or the South American caiman. Cases have been documented where the Nile crocodile stalked African women washing clothes in a river, charged a woman, seized her with its powerful jaws, and thrashed her to death by violently shaking its head and neck. Attacking our dugout might just seem like an appetizer, but, of course, I didn't know this at the beginning.

Mike and I would usually start the day by throwing a line with nothing more than a safety pin on it into the muddy-brown water. No sooner did the pin hit the water than a fish was pulled in. We'd fling it over, rope and all, to the cook, who slit it open and put it on a hot grill for our breakfast. It was delicious!

One day Mike started telling me about how his father, a combination farmer and hunter, had hunted river crocodile and how dangerous that type of hunt was. Next thing I knew I was saying, "Okay, let's take a shot at it ourselves." Mike took me seriously.

Crocodile-hunting is a nocturnal sport and you do it from a *mokoro* or dugout canoe built about sixteen feet long and about twelve to fourteen inches deep. It skims along on the top of the water away from the tall reeds and papyrus that line the steep banks. The boat was big enough for two of our camp boys to pole it from the back, while I lay at the bow of the boat with a .375 rifle. I was on my stomach to help steady the gun. Mike squatted behind me ready with his rifle, too.

We pulled out from shore side just as night had fallen. The air, as usual, was steamy, and as the light faded, it was like setting off into a mist. Despite the buzz of insects, it was so hot that none of us wore shirts.

Part of your hunter's job is to brief you on when to shoot and how to best place your shot. This time the advice that I got was to look for two red eyes skimming just above the shallow surface of the water and to aim for the midpoint between them.

Crocodiles are huge animals. Much broader than alligators and with lengths averaging over twenty feet long, they were considerably larger than the boat I was in. In fact, a swish from one of the beasts' tails could have cut the boat in half, leaving us all in some very strange water, so the object was not to miss. There was no leeway here. If you just wound the animal, he'll come right at you and your life won't be worth a damn until you kill him. That's why I said it's probably one of the dumbest things I've ever done in my life.

We had been poling the river silently for about an hour because we didn't want to alert any animals drinking at the water's edge. Then suddenly around a bend in the water I saw them—beady red eyes. One set belonged to a beast right in front of me that swam steadily at the boat as if it were his adversary. Knowing that my life could depend on it, I fired a shot into the right place. A .375 is a powerful rifle, so I probably shattered the crocodile's brain.

He lay dead in the water, thrashing his tail, and the boys poled the boat over to him and pushed his body over to the side. Making sure of where they were landing, they jumped ashore and pulled him up on the bank so they could return the next day to skin him. I had no interest in doing anything with the hide; I admire the pelts of different animals and enjoy looking at them, but I wasn't thinking in terms of crocodile shoes, bags, or belts so I was willing to let the boys have the skin and head.

I helped drag the crocodile ashore and saw he measured about twenty-one feet. When we returned to the camp, I was surprised to see the whole hunt had only taken about three hours. Something made it seem different from all the others I had been on, and I think the difference has to do with my love of stalking and my feeling that I hadn't really stalked my prey here. I had less mobility here in the dugout than I had when I normally went after game on foot, and instead of actively tracking spoor, I passively paddled down river waiting for my prey to come to me. Above all, in the bush I always felt I had some chance of survival in case anything happened; here on the river I felt I'd be good as dead if I ever fell overboard. The Chobe may be a shallow river, but for me it meant the chance of deep trouble, and I was glad when the hunt was over.

Chapter Six
Tribal Encounters

When you're in sales, it's very important to be able to "read" people correctly—to be alert to how sincere they seem and what tone their conversation takes. Tuning into these directional signals tells you whether or not you're going to receive an order. This same alertness is important when you're hunting big game also. I've been lucky because most of the time my "readings" have been correct and I've made the sale, but maybe this skill comes fairly easily to me because I've always been curious about people.

This natural curiosity made me want to know more about the native tribesmen I met in Africa. I don't pretend to be an anthropologist who's spent years studying one particular tribe, but I do think of myself as a keen observer of people—it's part of my overall alertness to my surroundings. I did live for a while in a Masai village; I travelled with Zulus for weeks at a time on safari; and twice, I believe, I was the first white American ever to be seen by groups of isolated, tribal people—Bushmen in the Kalahari Desert and Falasha Jews in northern Ethiopia. Getting glimpses into the lives and rituals of all these native people was as exciting to me as anything else in Africa; in a way, the insights I brought home with me were also a form of trophy-gathering.

On my first two safaris, I had been fascinated with stories I had heard about the Masai in East Africa, as parts of Kenya were still called. Taller and slimmer than other tribespeople, the Masais' copper-colored faces and erect posture had an almost aristocratic bearing. The Masai themselves, I was told, thought they were superior somehow to the Kikuyu and other tribes. They enjoyed a reputation for being "high and mighty" and for never catering to anyone, which included not working for the white man as gun-bearers, porters, cooks or camp boys. So although we hunted game near their reserves and traded with them, they never worked with us on safari.

This was the typical picture of the proud Masai—the *moran* or young warrior painted with red ocher clay and wrapped only in a shawl and a leather apron over his genitals, standing tall and graceful balanced on one leg with an aski or spear helping to support him. But on my second safari, I had seen another view of the Masai, which seemed much less noble; it was a picture of a tribe on the move towards new pasture grounds, leaving a weak, old man scrambling to keep pace with them until he fell behind and was attacked and killed by wild dogs. I tried to learn from the white hunter, who was with me at the time, not to judge the Masai by my own standards, but my interest in them was aroused by this episode and I became determined to find out more about them.

About three months before going back to Kenya on my third safari, I sent ahead some trinkets that I thought would help me gain favor with some of the Masai chieftains. My aim was to get their permission to live with them or close to their manyattas. The Masai are nomads and their temporary villages are made up of groups of manyattas or twig-and-dung-covered huts spaced out around a circular enclosure.

A Masai man has a hut for each of his wives, which average about three, and there's also a separate hut for men, which no women can enter. Because the Masai's wealth is in the size of his cattle herd, ideally, he wants one son and many daughters. That way he can receive cattle as a bride-price for his daughters, and with only one son, they can share the cattle herd and wealth advantageously. So important are cattle to Masai men that at night the cows are driven home where they stay in the protective enclosure of huts.

In making arrangements for this safari through letters, my white hunter, Bill Jenvey, had suggested that some small gifts might make the Masai react favorably to my request. At that time in the early 1960s, the Masai were not the modern and sophisticated people that they are today. Now, if someone even wants to take their picture, they put their hands out to collect some *schillingi* first. (The Kenyan schilling is the basic unit of currency.) But back then, they had no use for money, so I stocked up on a load of flashlights, small pocket knives, mirrors, gadgets, balloons, and postcards, and I sent it all over in advance.

These small novelties seemed like nothing to us, but they made a great impact on the Masai. Many of them had never seen themselves in a mirror or heard a balloon pop. I remember once that two Masai women wandered close to our parked Land Rover and became fascinated with the sideview mirror. As one of them looked in the mirror and saw her reflection, she turned around to her friend and said in Swahili, "That's you." I tried to convince her, by hand motions, that it was herself she was seeing, not her friend, because it was the first time she had ever seen her own reflection so clearly.

Once I arrived in Nairobi, I collected the shipment of trinkets, and Bill Jenvey and I set out for the

Serengeti Plain, one of the great open places of Africa that's rich with game. After travelling for a couple of days, we came across a Masai village. Bill indicated to the chief that I had gifts with me, and after some negotiations, the chief agreed to let us set up camp about thirty yards away from the main entrance to the village.

We used that camp as a base to hunt from, so although I never woke up in the morning and planned on deliberately spending the day in study of the Masai, just in the normal day of comings-and-goings I got to observe the Masai a lot and to mingle with them, using my hunter Bill as a translator. Most of the time, the Masai were distant, accepting me in their company when I visited their manyattas but not venturing forth into our camp. That may have been due to their feeling of arrogance, since the only restriction the chief imposed on us was to tell us to keep the black Africans in our camp from mingling with his tribe. Bill explained that it was because the Masai thought they were superior to everyone else.

Only a few young Masai were curious enough to wander around our tents, touching things that were strange to them. I remember once taking an outdoor bath, as was usual on safari, and being stared at by two Masai *morani* who probably wondered why the white man was taking a bath in water instead of anointing his body with animal fat and then covering it with ocher-colored clay the way they did. I never saw the Masai bathe, and I imagine that the fat and clay must have felt comfortable on their skin. I did notice that none of the Masai had any skin blemishes or problems, but I don't know if the clay contributed to that or not. I do know that their aroma wasn't always so pleasant, especially if you were standing downwind of them or visiting inside their smoky, dark huts.

I shared a little food with the Masai, eating a kind of liquid cornmeal paste with them before they added the cow's blood and urine to it which they were known for; I watched their women brew beer and sampled some of the fermenting mash; and I heard some of their folk legends. But of all the things I saw with the Masai, the experience that impressed me the most was the time I was privileged to watch a male circumcision.

As a circumcised man, I naturally had my own traumatic memories of the ritual—both unconsciously from my own experiences, I'm sure, and from seeing my son circumcised. But there's a difference between circumcising an eight-day-old infant, which is when Jewish boys undergo this procedure, and performing it on an adolescent boy! Among the Masai, young males mark the passage from being boys to morani or warriors between fourteen to sixteen years old, when they're deemed strong enough to withstand the ceremony. Usually, groups of boys are circumcised together, but the ceremony I saw involved only one young man.

The only word I can used to describe the event is "crude." The night before the young man had slept away from his family with his bachelor friends, and there had been singing, chanting, and I'm sure some drinking going on. Early in the morning, a crowd of men and a few women gathered in front of the hut where he'd be circumcised and the chanting resumed.

The young man was led forward, willingly, almost like a hero. He entered the hut and lay down on a mat of goat skins. An older men sat behind him and helped to support his head and neck. A group of his "friends" held his arms and legs on the ground, and a piece of wood was held across his mouth for him to bite on. The elder who was paid to do the circumcising held a very basic instrument made of a sharpened stone and used it to cut away the foreskin of the penis. The blood poured out, and they wrapped a leaf of some kind around the penis. When it was all over, a shout of glee came from everyone around him, inside and out of the hut.

I'm sure the pain must have been excruciating but throughout the whole procedure the boy held still, limp almost, and didn't utter a cry.

During the recovery period, the young boy is sent to live in another small camp with other newly circumcised morani until they are healed. Then, I was told, they have the privilege of moving from village to village to bed down with any available female. During this part of the initiation period, they learn to live in the bush and they slowly bond together until they try to kill a lion or a leopard with only their primitive metal-tipped spears and war staffs. The degree of bravery they show during the hunt is what establishes their separate identities and status within the tribe.

On a different occasion, I was allowed to watch the circumcision of a female but from a much greater distance than for the boy's circumcision. Only women were allowed in the hut where it took place, but from what I could gather, standing outside and looking through "big eyes" or binoculars through the spaces between all the women crowded in front of me, it seemed to be performed in the same crude manner as the first circumcision I had seen.

In this case, the object was to remove the clitoris because of the belief that without the clitoris a woman wouldn't have the feelings or passion for sex, so she'd be faithful to her husband while still remaining a candidate to produce children. But in spending time among the Masai, I couldn't help but observe that the girls who were circumcised at about age twelve to fourteen years old apparently had a considerable amount of scar tissue in their vaginas, which must have caused a lot of itching. I say this because it was not unusual to see a girl inserting a smooth stick into her vagina and using it to scratch herself. At other times, they seem to use the stick to masturbate. In fact, I think circumcision often made the girls want to have sex more because the penis probably does the same job as the stick.

If Masai women were expected to be just nonpassionate child-bearers after marriage, there was a different set of standards for them before they became wives. Quite often we'd be tracking across tall grass and hear laughter and other sounds coming from a group of young men and a girl who'd be having sex right out in the open. I gathered it was acceptable for five or six young morani to take along one or two of these girls who'd travel with them for many days, and the boys would make constant sexual use of them.

As part of the sexual attitudes of many of the African tribespeople, it was not unusual for me to be offered a native woman. We never had any women on safari, but I know often the blacks who worked with us would spend the night with women from nearby villages, although that didn't happen when we stayed at this Masai camp.

As for me, I may have looked hard at some of the bare-breasted women, but although sex was important to me when I was home with my wife, I can honestly say I was never tempted by any of the black African women. Sure, there may have been times when I tossed around with sleeplessness on my cot at night and was curious about African women, but as far as being seriously aroused by anything I saw, the answer is no. To speak like a white hunter, I travelled with a heavy load in my rifle, but my other rifle wasn't interested in shooting that kind of game!

In wandering around the Masai village, I also noticed that outside the main circle of huts an isolated, small twig hut had been built quite some distance away. When I asked about it, I was told that menstruating girls and women stayed there so their menstrual blood wouldn't contaminate anything. When females had their periods and were segregated from the tribe, they were completely unprotected except for some sticks and loud noise-makers. Often the women became prey to predatory animals, who were attracted to them by the odor they emitted. Once when we returned from hunting, we noticed a flurry in the manyatta outside the village. It seems that some hyenas had tried to attack a menstruating woman but had been chased away.

The Masai in this particular village were affable enough, but a different group of them on a later safari proved to be the only Africans I ever had any trouble with. The Kikuyus left us alone despite the Mau Mau uprising in Kenya, nor did the Zulus ever show any resentment as whites. But the Masai, perhaps out of belief in their own superiority, saw fit to make fun of me; and the hunter I was travelling with had a philosophy of never letting African natives laugh at him or any other white person, especially when it's done with hostility, as seemed to be the case in this episode.

My professional hunter on this safari was a short, heavy-chested Rhodesian. We were hunting in the remote, dry plains of northern Kenya, a little below Lake Rudolf or Lake Turkana as it's called now. After being out for almost three weeks, we had to stock up on some supplies, like canned food and petrol, so the hunter and I took the Land Rover and drove about eight or ten miles to a native-owned trading post. It was nothing more than a fenced-in area about twenty-five or thirty yards square with a wooden store and a small warehouse. While he went in to make the purchase, I wandered around outside.

In front of the store, six Masai were standing and talking. As usual, they were balanced on one leg, like storks, leaning on their *askis* or spears. Now, the Masai were normally a somber people. It's rare that I've seen them look happy, but all of them looked at me, and one of them said something and they all started to laugh. I couldn't tell what they were saying, but it was obvious I was the object of their laughter.

With this, my professional hunter came out of the store. He was no taller than five foot four, but he was built broad and muscular and was powerful as hell. He listened to the Masai for a minute, and his ruddy face got black as anger surged up in it.

"Clout him," he shouted to me. "Clout him or *I'll kill the son of a bitch!*" With this, he went for his sidearm. The Masai who had been talking about me seemed nearly seven feet tall, and he had a spear. But having spent some time with my hunter, I knew if I didn't hit this Masai, he would put a shot in him.

Now it's hard to hit someone you're not mad at, but I knew I had to put the Masai away with one blow. I moved in quickly to the Masai and hit him as hard as

I could on the side of his jaw. He dropped to the ground! With this, the other Masai just disappeared. I turned to the hunter and asked him what the hell that was all about.

"The Masai was telling a story about you and it was disrespectful," he said. "The Masai said your mouth looked like a woman's vagina."

At first, that didn't make any sense to me. But then I realized that Masai males are always hairless. Many men and even some women go as far as shaving their heads. I, on the other hand, normally have a moustache, and since I had been out in the bush for three weeks, I had also let my beard grow. To them, I guess, my red lips showing in the middle of all that facial hair must have reminded them of a woman's genitals.

I was amused by the comparison, since it never would have occurred to me, but my hunter found it insulting; and when you're travelling with a professional white hunter, you trust him to be your interpreter and your guide to behavior.

I don't assume to know enough history or anthropology to be able explain why the Masai generally acted as haughty as they did. I do know, however, that another tribe of African warriors, the Zulus of South Africa, were almost the exact opposite toward me when I employed them on safaris.

The Zulus were fighters also, a tribe feared by other natives in nineteenth-century South Africa and respected by the British, whom they fought in 1879. The Zulus are the most numerous of the Bantu-speaking people, and they're very well-organized and maybe that gives them a sense of security. I respect all the African tribes I came in contact with, but the people I like best are the Zulus. They are powerful and strong, especially the men, and they're not surly when they work for you. On safari, I found them to make the most effort to understand and protect the client.

One Zulu and one episode particularly stand out in my mind. It was during my second-to-last safari between 1977–1978 while we were hunting in the Transvaal or the northeastern part of South Africa. Perhaps because I was the oldest man in the party, being sixty-three years old, one of the Zulus with us particularly watched out for me. He wasn't very young himself, probably in his forties and a kind of chief to his own group, but he had been brought up to respect elders, and he probably recognized my age before I even did.

His name was Kuba Saba, which I learned meant "the day the cow died," since apparently that's what happened to one of his father's cows on the day he was born. Kuba Saba was my gun-bearer, and a close, comfortable relationship existed between us. He seemed to have my welfare at heart more than any other person I ever met on safari. Yet it was done in a manly way, so I never felt coddled, which I wouldn't have tolerated. He just anticipated things I might need or want done the way someone might if he had spent years working alongside you. On this particular trip, for example, we spent a lot of time on horseback, and if we tried to ford a stream, Kuba Saba would be right there beside my horse, holding the bridle, so there'd be no stumbling over the heavily stoned bottom.

Kuba Saba liked to hum and sing around camp, a habit my mother had while she worked around the house and which I picked up also. He had a beautiful voice, which I understand is not unusual with the

Zulus, so I used to encourage him to sing songs from his tribe.

Because I liked the songs so much, somewhere along the line I must have asked through Rob Dean, my hunter, if Kuba Saba could bring some of his tribe to our camp and stage a Zulu song-and-dance fest for us. We were camping near Kuba Saba's *shamba* or village, and I don't know how far it was, but I know that every night he'd hike back to sleep with one of his wives and then return to us by breakfast, which was about sunrise.

I had read about these colorful tribal songfests, but I had never seen one that wasn't staged to entertain tourists. Unlike the Masai, whom I had had to warm up with advance gifts, at no time do I remember offering to pay Kuba Saba or give him or his tribe anything for this special favor. It was just a simple request, a casual comment made in conversation one day and I didn't know if it would be granted or not.

One night awhile after I had made my request, we were sitting around the campfire after dinner when off in the distance, I saw torches burning in a single line, with about 150–200 people marching toward camp. With surprise, I realized that Kuba Saba, who had never indicated to me whether it would be possible for me to see a Zulu festival, had taken it upon himself as chief of his tribe to grant my wish. The torches were set off against the pitch black night, and as the Zulus came closer, I could hear the sound of harmonizing, with male voices carrying the main tune while the females did the back-up singing.

As they arrived in camp, the Zulus started a slow, rhythmic march around our campfire while continuing to sing. There were maybe about a hundred men, and the rest were women and children, who sang harmony with the men. Some of the adult men wore feathered headdresses and had their faces and bodies painted, but many of them just wore the kind of Western-style hand-me-downs you find for sale all over Africa. At times, the songs and the marching speeded up. Their feet beat out the rhythm on the hard-packed dirt, and there was the tinkling noise made by bells sewn onto leather straps and wrapped around their ankles and wrists. But overpowering everything was the sound of their voices blending together.

The campfire was flickering, the table that night had been set with a white linen tablecloth, the Zulus were holding their torches high, and it was like being given a royal command performance of a marvelous choral group. It was raw, authentic, and very moving because it was obvious that they were honoring me.

Our cook, a Bantu named Jackson, must have been in on the surprise because he brought out a huge cake that had some fruit in it that tasted like apple. We ate many other delicacies as the Zulus danced and sang, but they only accepted some of our beer and alcohol—not much for that large group really, when you consider we had only brought two bottles of hard booze with us.

The concert lasted for about two-to-three hours, and then the Zulus disappeared as mysteriously as they had come. I have no idea how far they had to walk to us and then back home again, but it was fascinating to hear the music and see the torchlights fade in the distance. I was totally grateful to them for putting on this songfest, and there was nothing I could do to show them how I felt other than just say "Thank you" in English. Money would have had no value to them out in the bush, and I had nothing material to give them. Besides, I think it would have offended their dignity. Kuba Saba and I were friends, and you don't "pay" friends for favors. When our safari ended, I did give him a lot of my clothes, but I like to think what he really appreciated was the surprise and satisfaction on my face the night of the songfest and the way I spoke to his people afterward.

If some of my encounters with African tribesmen had been initiated by hiring them to make up the safaris, my experience with the Bushmen was entirely spontaneous. I was hunting in Botswana, formerly known as Bechuanaland, when my footsteps literally crossed those of this Stone-Age tribe. It took place around 1971, shortly after the country became independent from Britain and before the big onset of tourism by sports hunters and photographic-safari types. The Bushmen are one of the world's last hunter-gatherer tribes, and they were still living remote from Western civilization, in the safety of the deep Kalahari Desert, when I met them.

My hunter, Ronnie Blackbeard, and I were hunting out of Serowe, on the eastern edge of the Kalahari Desert. Now, the Kalahari isn't your Hollywood desert with wave after wave of sand dunes. It's a dry basin covering about two hundred thousand square miles of scrubland with tufts of grasses and trees. Tall termite mounds break up the horizon in some spots, and there are some deep underground wells.

One day, we were tracking tsessebe, a medium-sized, dark red antelope, and the herd was moving farther away from us and deeper into the desert. Because it was getting late in the afternoon, we decided to camp out rather than return to our base camp. As darkness fell, we noticed a small fire burning and moving midway between us and the horizon. Rather than a hallucination brought about by spending too much time in the desert sun, Ronnie explained the light probably came from a torch being carried by some Bushmen. He was excited because, although he had been born in Botswana, he had never seen a real aborigine before. I guess his excitement was contagious because the next thing I knew I suggested we find out if they really were Bushmen.

We started out on foot to follow the flame, using only Ronnie's sense of direction and inner map of the landscape to guide us. I don't remember even planning what we would say or do if we made contact with the group. Finally, we got within about five hundred yards of them and saw what appeared to be a small family. But they were aware of some moving objects following them, so they kept moving away from us. Because it was nightfall and we were getting farther into the desert, we decided to return to camp and see if we could find the group again in the morning.

Daybreak came and we climbed into our open-sided Land Rover and picked up the trail of the group. Once we spotted them, we left the vehicle and approached them on foot. As we got closer, we noticed that there was a man and woman, a young girl, and a suckling baby. The man had a wiry strength to him, but he seemed less than five feet tall; the woman and child were much smaller and none of them seemed that well fed. Later, Ronnie told me that the Bushmen survive by eating wild beans, roots, and nuts, and by hunting game. Occasionally, they gather honey from hives and in times of drought they rely on wild melons for nourishment and liquids.

This particular family group had somehow gotten separated from their band. Usually, I was later told, ten or fifteen people will travel together over territory that varies with the wet and dry season. The Bushmen we met were all naked, and their skin was a grayish color, probably, I guess, from the fine, gritty sand that stuck to them as well as from the salt evaporating from their sweat. The man wore a leather belt from which hung a sharpened stone, but that was the only weapon or tool we could see.

As we moved toward them, we observed that the woman was puffing a leaf that was loosely rolled up. Occasionally, she would pass it to the man and even to the young girl. I've never smoked myself, but I've heard it takes the edge off hunger, so maybe that's why they all shared the leaf. We could tell from the way they stood still waiting for us that they were afraid and so we slowed our approach. Since Ronnie smoked and smoking seemed to be a mutual area of communication, we decided that he would approach them alone while I stayed about ten yards back.

Holding a newly lit, filter-tip cigarette between his fingers, Ronnie walked the last few feet between them and us. The Bushman put his arm out, reached for the cigarette, and put it to his mouth. He inhaled briefly, then without exhaling, inhaled again for a longer time. The power of his lungs was so great that the cigarette burned down to the filter in almost an instant!

While all this was going on, a large herd of tsessebe came into view until they were grazing about one-half mile away from us. Once he had established that we weren't a threat to his family and he could give his attention back to the herd, the male took off after them. He didn't run as if he were racing, but he ran at a steady trot, especially once he singled out an animal who broke away from the herd.

He chased after the animal for almost forty-five minutes, gaining on him slowly. Both of them kept running round and round in circles until the animal literally dropped in exhaustion. By this time, they were about a hundred yards away from us, so we could see the man sit on the animal and twist its neck until the bone broke and the animal died. Then, he took the stone knife, cut the belly open, tore out the insides, slung the animal, weighing about 125 pounds, across his shoulders, and trotted back to us.

It seemed like a tremendous load to me, especially since he was such a little man, but he came back barely winded from the experience. While this hunt had been going on, the woman had kindled a fire with some sticks she carried in a bundle. Then we all squatted down together and waited for the man to return. There was no conversation between us because she and Ronnie shared no common language, nor was there much we could say with hand gestures.

While I understand the Bushmen have a language based on a clicking of the tongue to the palate, at no time did I hear anything resembling a word while we were with the family. I assume from this and other observations I made that this particular group lived remote and isolated from other Bushmen groups, who occasionally come into contact with white men and pick up a few words of language from them. I also guess that these Bushmen we met had never seen a white person before. Ronnie was so elated that he could hardly wait to get back to tell his father about the experience!

Once the man returned, he threw the animal down,

and the woman, the girl, and he began tearing at the flesh near the rump and ate it raw. Only after they had consumed a sizable amount did they cut up half-inch strips of meat and drape them over a line hanging over the fire. I suppose they were drying it like biltong or dried beef jerky.

Throughout this whole time, the group ignored us and surprisingly didn't offer us any meat. It was as if they didn't know what to make of us, so they pretended we just weren't there. In a way, the experience was comparable to watching Japanese Kabuki theatre or seeing foreign actors perform an unfamiliar play in a language you don't speak. You don't understand quite everything you see or hear, but it's still interesting to watch. Meeting the Bushmen was especially thrilling for Ronnie and me, who both loved hunting, because it was a once-in-a-lifetime chance to see how our primitive ancestors killed game bare-handed with nothing more than Stone-Age weapons.

When I talk about the Bushmen being "primitive" or coming from the "Stone Age," I'm not being condescending. Some archaeologists, I'm told, believe the Bushmen have lived in the Kalahari Desert for about twenty-five thousand years. They base this belief on a series of rock paintings found on the walls of caves and rocky outcroppings in the northern Kalahari Desert. As happens often on safaris, you sometimes find yourself doing things you never anticipate doing. That's how I came to explore a cave in the Kalahari.

This time I was on an open hunt with Mike Rundgren; we had nothing specific in mind, but we were near the northern edge of the Kalahari, an area bordered with vast swamplands and forest near the Chobe River. Because the region was full of large herds of giraffes, hippo, and rhino in addition to antelopes and gazelle, we planned to be out for about three weeks.

We moved around a lot, and at one point Mike told me that we were near a part of the desert where he had once come across a cave. He had spotted it on an earlier safari, but he hadn't ventured into it because both he and his client had thought it would be too dangerous. Entering a cave is always risky, especially when there's a strong chance that it's home for predatory animals. Even a small animal like a field mole or a dik dik who may be hiding from the sun in there could startle you and cause you to injure yourself somehow.

But there we were in the part of the Kalahari where Mike remembered having come across the entrance to the cave, and on a whim, I insisted that we look for it and go inside. The cave was part of an outcrop of rocks about twenty-five feet high, but the entrance was almost buried in sand that had been piled up by winds and left undisturbed. Because we knew that caves of this type could be home for animals, we decided to wait for nightfall and go in with searchlights. That way, whatever animals were inside would be blinded by the light and we would see them before they saw us.

When dusk fell, we ventured very cautiously into the entrance of the cave. We didn't have the support of our gun-bearers, although we did carry shotguns with us. Not having encountered any large beasts in the first few yards, we gathered up the courage to move farther into the cave. Coming in from the extreme dryness of the desert, we found the air to be musty and dank, almost as if there was some underground source of water nearby.

As we progressed about thirty to forty yards into the cave, we could feel the ground slant downward.

There were a good many small animals inside that looked like they belonged to the wild dog or jackal family, but they scurried past us to get to the entrance of the cave. Once we reached the center of the cave, we were able to stand up in a chamber that must have been about eight to ten feet high. Our flashlights hit a large expanse of wall where we could make out some dim traces of paintings. A closer inspection showed stick figures of Bushmen very scantily dressed chasing after a herd of springbok or grey duiker, two types of small and medium-sized antelope found in the area. The paintings were faded, with ocher or brownish-red being the main color, but the outlines of the animals were quite clear and recognizable.

After checking out the longitude and the latitude of the cave's location, we subsequently advised the *National Geographic* magazine, which eventually sent a team to photograph the inside of the cave. While it may not have been a monumental archaeological discovery or a huge accomplishment, the danger of our initial movement into the cave will always remain with me.

Another experience that will also remain with me was meeting some of the black Jews of Ethiopia before it became fashionable to speak of them as Falashas. I was hunting mountain nyala, a scarce, spiral-horned antelope found only in the high lands of Ethiopia, with Thomas Mattanovich. He was a displaced Yugoslavian who had settled in Ethiopia, become a professional game hunter, and married a black woman who served as our cook on safari.

It was near the end of Haile Selassie's reign as emperor in 1974. I remember the time so well because the hotel I stayed at in Addis Ababa was bombed by rebels when I was there, but fortunately they chose to blow up a different side of the hotel than the one I was on.

On some safaris that covered lots of territory, I would take a small plane, known as a "jump" plane, to get from one area to another. My hunter would fly with me while the safari personnel, vehicles, tentage, etc., followed us on land, usually arriving a day or two later.

On one of these particular trips, I noticed a magazine with a picture of a black man with Semitic features who had a large Star of David hanging from his neck. The magazine was written in Ethiopian, a language I could not read; but because I was interested in the story, I took the magazine, stuck it in my knapsack, and forgot about it. Later on, I found out the story was about a black Hewbrew tribe in Ethiopia who claimed their existence and heritage came from the Queen of Sheba.

Our safari went well, and when I had taken the "bag" I was licensed for, I still had about a week before leaving for home. I dug out the story and asked Tom about it, but he said he had never heard about this particular tribe. But I didn't give up, and after some more inquiries, I learned that the tribe lived in the very northern part of Ethiopia in the Gondar province, wedged in between the desert of Sudan and the mountains of Eritrea.

The distance was about 150 miles from us, and the map showed no paved roads to take us there. Now, in all my years of going to Africa, being Jewish had never seemed particularly important to me. I had gotten to know some Jewish people in South Africa, but that was more social than anything else. Still, I was determined to find out about these black Ethiopian Jews, so we

With wife and children at the Jarkows' Florida home

Transportation often used on African safaris

Author greeting Prime Minister Shamir of Israel

Meeting with president of Mexico, Carlos Salinas de Gortari

Nobel prize winner Elie Weisel congratulating author on his 75th birthday

U.S. Vice President Dan Quayle with Mr. Jarkow in 1989

Being congratulated by Joe Brennen, Maine's governor (far left), at the ground breaking of Kent Co. plant in Fort Kent, Maine, about 1979

Helicopter used in searching out Guatemalan Indian refugee camps

President Ankara of Panama, one of many government officials visited after having replaced Noriega

Bocaire A.D.L. Committee 1990 (missing, B. Hewitt)

took off for the remote, highland villages they called home.

Tom and I loaded the Land Rover for provisions for about five or six days; we took no weapons because we had taken whatever "bag" we were licensed for and we wanted to alleviate any fear from people we might meet on the way to Eritrea. At that time the area was so isolated that there was no danger from any organized rebels.

We drove across extremely rough terrain for about a day-and-a-half until we came to a deeply rutted trail that was obviously for animal-drawn wagons. We were climbing up mountains whose height I would not guess at, but although the nights were cold, the heat of the day made travel comfortable.

As we got to a high level of mountains, we encountered the first signs of this black Semitic tribe, an armed guard carrying an ancient-looking but still serviceable rifle. The Falashas, or "strangers" as the Ethiopians call them, carried guns because of the threat of sudden attack from neighbors or from royal government landlords who ruled like medieval dukes. The guard wore a long, black gown with a wide-brimmed circular hat. Silently, he waved us on.

As we moved higher into the mountains, we met more groups of people similarly dressed. They were black but their features were long, thin, sharp, and entirely different from any other black tribe I had seen in Africa. Except for the color of their skin, their facial characteristics were unmistakably Hebrew! They weren't friendly, but they did not deter us once we showed them that we had no weapons.

Finally, we reached a main village of what seemed like four or five hundred people, who lived in stone houses off narrow alleyways. Apparently, the people lived off farming and trading. On our approach to the village, about twenty-five to thirty men came out to us and indicated that we were *not* welcome. I showed them again that we carried no weapons and I even tried to convince them I was Jewish too, but I failed miserably in that attempt. I knew no Yiddish nor any Hebrew; and as I later learned, even if I had spoken the language of the Bible, it wouldn't have done any good since the Falashas spoke and prayed in their native language, Amharic. Tom suggested jokingly that I drop my pants to prove I was a circumcised Jew, but I wasn't prepared to go that far!

Finally, though, we must have convinced them we were harmless, and they allowed us to walk around the village. At the end of one alley, built into the mountain wall, I noticed an entrance with the Star of David hammered above it. There was a crude wooden table in the middle with a cloth on it and a small parchment scroll was lying on it. Obviously, my arrival had disturbed the group that had been there. I couldn't get close enough to the scrolls to see what was on them, and, truthfully, even if I had I wouldn't have been able to read anything.

Up until this point, we had not seen any women, which I thought was strange. But as we walked back to the Land Rover, three women came out of a building, walking huddled over in their dark shawls. Probably most of the people had been too frightened by our unexpected arrival.

It would be nice to say that seeing these people gave me a shock of recognition, that I had found my own people. But that's not true. I went out of my basic curiosity about people, and having seen these dark-skinned Jews, I realized I had come across a group that few people in the outside world even knew about. Having done what I set out to do, I put the Falashas in the back of my mind until Israel began taking them by boat and air out of Ethiopia to Israel in 1984–1985. I realized then that I had been an observer to something that was frankly historic.

I wanted very much to take part physically in Operation Moses, as this modern exodus was called, but at age seventy, I was considered too old to help. However, I managed to be a pretty good financial contributor to the effort.

I've always felt that I was a man of action, an adventurer almost, more than a philosopher or a man of thought. At least, that's the side of me that came out when I went on safari in Africa. It's only been lately that I've realized the implications of all that I've done and seen, and I wish that I had thought to ask more questions about things back then.

But even when you think you know something about people, something new happens and teaches you that you still have lessons to learn. That's the point, I guess, of this last little episode about the good missionary.

It was during the mid-1960s and many African countries were trying to carve out their independence either through peaceful means or by force. With Botswana, for instance, nationhood came easily and quietly; with Kenya and Rhodesia, it came after many bloody battles. Other smaller, more contained battles were also being fought by different tribes, but somehow politics remained remote when we were out in the bush. I heard stories about safaris going out with armed guards, but I felt safe. I knew my men. After all,

I trusted my white professional hunter, and he must have trusted the blacks he hired, so what could go wrong?

We had made camp one night somewhere in northern Rhodesia. In the middle of the night, I was awakened by a noise, and by the time I had checked my shoes for scorpions and slipped them on, my hunter was already outside talking to six black militiamen. They had come to take away two of our camp boys. When I asked what they had done, my hunter told me this story.

The camp boys, whose tribal group I don't remember, came from southern Rhodesia where they had been accused of killing a white missionary. The woman belonged to a German mission, and for about four years, she had medically cared for the tribe and taught them hygiene and birth control. She was good to the them and they loved her, I was told. So much did the tribe love her for her goodness that one night they got drunk at some festival and decided to keep some of her goodness with them always by killing her and then eating her. Six people, in particular, were accused of the murder, and two of them had been working for us.

The militia had tracked them to our camp and were taking the two men back with them. They left in the dark of night; after they had travelled less than a mile from us, I heard a couple of shots and I don't know whether the men ever got to stand trial or not. But the episode did remind me that you can't ever say you really know people and that you can't relax your basic alertness to what's going on around you.

Chapter Seven
From Boy Scout to Nazi Hunter

Getting ready to put on my "Boy Scout clothes" was what I always thought of whenever I packed my old shirts, sweaters, shorts, and khaki bush jackets for Africa. My hunting clothes were a contrast to the tailored business suits I normally wore, and they stood for the different life-style I led in Africa—days and nights full of adventure and camping out with the boys. But my safari days also gave me the chance to do something I had done occasionally before—to jump into situations to help people.

This impulse to come to the rescue or to correct wrongs always seemed instinctive in me, even in my youth. I rarely get even verbally mad, but twice as a young man in Brooklyn, I got into fights—once when some punks in a car, stopped at a traffic light on Ocean Parkway, began insulting Edna, who was very pregnant with Joan, our first child, and again when a crowd of Italian guys had encircled an old Jewish man and were pushing him around, making anti-Semitic remarks.

In both cases, I would not have been able to live with myself if I did not take action. Blows were delivered each time, but I think I gave a good account of myself. In the first case, I plowed right into the guys in the car until some others pulled me back and the car drove off. The second time, I stepped into the circle and put myself between the old man and his attackers and told them to take me on instead. Onlookers from across the street began to gather around, and the man managed to slip away safely in the crowd while most of the thugs faded away until only one was left. There was name-calling, a few body feints and jabs, and he threatened me with a knife, but finally he backed down too.

Even when I was middle-aged, I never backed away from a fight if the cause was just. Once I took off after a purse-snatcher during a crowded lunch hour in the Garment District because I heard a woman screaming for help. I caught up with the guy and held him until the police came.

Another time, when I was in my sixties, an unruly young man began cursing a driver and passengers on a city bus I was riding. I tapped him with my umbrella and asked him to leave, and next thing I knew the bus had stopped and we were rolling out the steps into the street, where some people pulled us apart. The funny thing about both incidents was the look of surprise on people's faces when they saw me—well-groomed and suited with a tie on, looking eminently respectable—getting involved in a physical brawl.

So even without Boy Scout clothes, I guess I tried to help out whenever I felt needed. But in Africa that tendency was carried out from the extremes of simply helping out people to actually participating in a full-blown mission to track down and kill a Nazi war criminal.

Sometimes being a "Boy Scout" in the bush meant simply sharing what you had with people who were lost or in need. That's what happened in the late 1970s when a now famous TV actress and her male companion got lost and found our camp in the Kalahari Desert.

It was just before nightfall when we noticed some lights off in the distance where none should be. Now, it's a weird thing, but out in the desert, at least in Botswana, there's no horizon. Instead of the land and the sky meeting at a point or on a line in the distance, there's just open space. Apparently, it has to do with ozone or the air mixtures, I've been told, but anyway, in that open space, we saw these lights, which had to belong to some vehicle because they couldn't have been brush fires or anything else.

The lights moved slowly, but eventually a Land Rover came into our camp, carrying a professional hunter, who turned out to know my hunter, another tall man who stepped out first, and a beautiful, young lady. It was about 10:00 P.M., as black as it can get out in the middle of the desert, and she had been asleep in the front seat. They had gotten lost and seen our campfires burning.

Once the couple was introduced to us, I immediately recognized the woman's name because her father was well known in show business. Her companion was introduced as some kind of European count, but she called him Caroll. We invited them to join us at the mess table and to spend time with us. That called for some rearrangements because I had my own tent, my hunter had his, and there were about five or six smaller tents for the various tribes that were with us. But we all shifted around. The two hunters moved into my tent and gave the actress and her friend my hunter's tent. There was only one cot in it—about twenty-seven inches wide and twelve inches above the floor—and as I lay in my own cot that night, I wondered how the two of them were going to fit into it, especially since the Count was six foot three inches tall.

In the morning, they asked if they could use our camp as a base. Since hospitality is one of the first rules of the bush, we agreed. Food wasn't a problem because we could always shoot for the pot, and since there were no complaints about the bed situation, they stayed with us for about five days. It was the only time on safari I ever saw silk panties hung out on the line to dry with the rest of our laundry.

Usually, the Count and his hunter would go off in their Land Rover between 4:30–5:00 A.M., when we also broke camp to begin our day's hunting. The actress would go off on foot with one of the blacks to take photographs in the bush, since she apparently was an avid photographer. Later, we'd meet and talk over the fire and I came to know and like her. But the Count was something else—he was arrogant and pompous to us and especially nasty to the blacks working with us. It showed up not only in his tone of voice but even to the point of being physically abusive to the blacks, and I finally told him off.

Sometime after they left, I ran into the young lady at a hotel in Victoria Falls; the Count was about to go back to his wife and children in Europe, and she asked if I wanted to go to Zanzibar with her since I had been there a few years before and we had talked about the country in camp.

Jokingly, I said, "You know, according to my religion, Orthodox Jewish brides have to soak in a mikvah or bath to cleanse themselves before entering into marriage. Because you've been with that bastard, you'd have to spend two weeks in a mikvah before I'd go with you."

Years later, I ran into her in New York; I was with Edna and she was with her husband. But we looked at each other and said, "Africa," and we both remembered.

Other times in Africa, helping out meant coming to someone's physical assistance. That happened twice—once when a South African farmer was threatened by baboons and a second time when Joy Adamson, author of *Born Free* and other books, was at risk of harm from the black Africans who worked for her.

It was just before nightfall, while we were hunting in a desolate part of the Drakensberg Mountains of South Africa, when a black runner reached our camp with news that the couple whose land we were hunting on were being threatened by a commando of baboons. In South Africa, all big-game hunting is done on private lands, so we had made arrangements to hunt on the property of an elderly farmer, who owned about 250,000 acres of land in the mountains that ran from near the Mozambique border to the south.

Although he was a big landowner, he also had a large family with eleven children, none of whom lived at home, and his house was surprisingly primitive. Standing at the base of a mountain, it was made of stone, with no electricity or indoor plumbing, and cooking was done in a separate shack on a wood-burning stove. The farmer and his wife even slept on a straw-filled mattress covered with a cotton quilt. Their income came from raising about twenty thousand sheep, who were held at the time in a corral.

We paid the farmer an agreed fee for the use of his land and then set off on horseback to scout for a good place to camp. In the night a black helper came to our camp, which was a three-hour ride from their house. He told us that the day before a huge commando of baboons had raided the sheep corral near the farmhouse and had killed some sheep and carried them off. Apparently, the baboons had gotten a taste for lamb when the herd was put out to pasture and had even raided the corral a few times before.

Wild baboons are not like the cute chimps you see tamed in circuses, and like many animals who become predators, they have excellent memories. The chacma baboons who inhabited this rocky region of South Africa live in groups of about ten to two hundred and are ruled by several large males, who each weigh as much as ninety pounds, I later learned.

These baboons were drawn to the sheep by their scent, and the sheep, in turn, were very sensitive to the scent of the baboons and would emit an enormous amount of "baaing" when they knew that the baboons were nearby. Although the elderly couple had been able to protect themselves by barricading the house, the situation had become dangerous and they asked us to help them get rid of the baboons.

We rode back on horseback, and about a mile away from the house, we dismounted in order not to let the horses' scent alert the baboons in the vicinity. It was about 2:00 A.M., and we had to plan how we'd discourage the baboons from ever invading the corral again. Since they were coming down from the top of mountain and had to pass through a narrow path that led down to the corral, we decided to wait for them.

Our plan put me about sixty yards up the mountain, with my hunter about fifteen to twenty yards behind me. He told me it would be necessary to kill the lead baboon or else it would be chaos, with as many as eighty baboons overwhelming us and moving toward their object, which was the sheep. Since I had never observed a pack of baboons in the wild, much less when they were on the run, I asked how I could pick out the leader. "Once they start gathering about two hundred yards above us, it'll be very obvious who the leader is," my hunter told me.

As the sun started to come up, we heard thunderous noises coming from the sheep below us in the corral. Before we had sighted the baboons, the sheep had smelled them and alerted us. Looking through my field glasses, I quickly picked out the lead baboon—a big grayish-brown fellow with a long ruff or collar of hair that stood straight up on end all around his neck. He was actually urging eight-to-ten of the largest baboons into what was an attack or "commando" team. Male baboons are known to be fierce fighters, using their long, sharp teeth as weapons, and this formation was proof of their fighting experience.

As they started to form, they began running down the crevice toward the bottom, where I lay in wait for him. Having armed myself with a shotgun instead of a rifle, I had the advantage of stopping the lead animal more easily. The wide range of a shotgun blast ensures a better chance of hitting the animal. As the commandos started moving toward me, I held my breath until the leader was about twenty yards away. The first shot blasted him and with that, the whole group of baboons fled back into the mountains.

As soon as they disappeared, the sheep quieted down. My hunter and I walked down to the base of the mountain toward the old couple's home, while our gun-bearers retrieved our horses and brought them to us. The couple thanked us in Afrikaans—a mixture of Dutch and other languages—and the old man insisted that he wanted to show me something special. He was adamant that I had to come alone because he wanted me, a foreigner, to see some property he prided himself on owning. But he would not consider showing it to a South African because he wanted knowledge of the property to stay only with himself and his oldest son.

I followed him on horseback for about two miles until the brush got too heavy for our horses, so we dismounted and walked for another quarter-mile. At this point, the brush got even thicker, so we both dropped to our hands and knees and started crawling underneath the low trees and brambles as if we were going into a cave. After fifty yards, we suddenly came into a white, sandy opening that was extremely bright. The light was so blinding that it hurt my eyes, but after adjusting to the glare, I realized I was in a petrified forest with massive white tree trunks and limbs lying on the ground like scattered cordwood. Everything—the ground, trees, and bushes—was bathed in a pure white light.

It was the first time I was ever in a petrified forest, and it was astonishing! I would estimate I was looking at a piece of land that was a million years old, and I was moved by the strange landscape. After wandering around, I asked if I could take a memento and we found a twenty-five pound piece of tree limb and tied it to my horse's saddle. When we returned, the old man made me promise that I would never reveal the location of the forest, and I never did. As far as I know, only the oldest of his children still knows its location. About three or four months after I came home, I also got a thank-you letter from one of the man's daughters; she wrote that the sheep had never been bothered by the baboons again.

Sometimes, it's not animals that threaten human life in Africa but people. That was the case on Joy

Adamson's farm on one of my safaris in the mid-1970s. We were on a hunt in southern Kenya when word reached us by courier that there was a revolt among the workers at the Adamsons' farm, and they were surrounded and being confined to their own house. Apparently, the "bush wireless" had told them we were in the area and they sought our help.

Joy Adamson had become quite famous for raising a lion cub and writing a book about it, *Born Free*. I didn't know too much about her or her husband at the time, but my professional hunter Pookie Darlow did. Since the situation was potentially a dangerous one, Pookie and I and two of our gun-bearers took off immediately for the farm in a Land Rover. When we got there in the middle of the afternoon, we found twenty or thirty Africans parading back and forth and shouting in dispute outside the perimeter of the stone house. They hadn't yet broken through the wooden fence and gate that surrounded the Adamsons' home, but they were getting themselves all charged up to do so.

In fact, they were making so much noise that they hardly noticed our presence until we got within a few hundred yards of the entrance to the farm and fired some shots in the air. Since they could see we were much more heavily armed than they were, they quickly dispersed and we entered the house.

The Adamsons were there, together with a few of their more loyal employees. Mrs. Adamson was tall; she moved in a very haughty manner and had a very caustic personality. I didn't know all the details of the dispute, but I gathered that it just involved her being plain rotten to her help. We stayed around for an hour to make sure the group of blacks remained dispersed, and as a "thank-you" gift, she gave me two of her prints of African natives.

Joy Adamson was a talented painter of plants and different tribesman, and she did a lot for wildlife conservation. But she herself suggested in one of her books, which I later read, that she had more patience with animals than with people, and I'd have to agree with her. I didn't really either like her or dislike her, but she had been in trouble and the tendency is always to jump in to help people who are in trouble.

Until my close involvement with the Anti-Defamation League, which came many years later, probably the fullest expression of my "Boy Scout" tendency came about when a South African Jewish friend persuaded me to take part in a mission to assassinate a Nazi war criminal hiding out in the Brazilian jungle.

Indirectly, it all began when I took a high fever after being bitten by an insect on one of my safaris to South Africa in early 1960s. My hunter made arrangements to have me flown to Durban where I was hospitalized for a few days. When Durban's Jewish community learned an American Jew was laid up, many came to visit with me and I made some good friends.

One of them was an older man, a fairly well-off financier who had his primary residence in Johannesburg. We kept up a correspondence, and I visited him on some of my subsequent safaris to South Africa. After finishing up a safari to Botswana in the mid-1960s, I had returned to my Johannesburg hotel where I found a message from him, asking me to call him immediately upon my arrival. Although I had just driven eight-and-a-half hours in a Land Rover and was dead tired, I phoned him and learned he wanted to see me right away. It was about 9:30 P.M., so I asked if we could postpone our meeting until the morning when I would be refreshed from a good night's sleep. But he said he had a "task" to ask me and he wanted me to "sleep on his request" before answering him.

He sounded so mysterious and so urgent that he persuaded me to visit him. Thirty minutes later his black chauffeur arrived in a vintage Rolls Royce. That in itself was surprising, since normally blacks were barred from being in Johannesburg after dark, so obviously my friend must have had some special connections.

Upon arriving at his home, he immediately took me into his library and told me he'd like me take part in a mission to search out a known Nazi who was living in the area of Mato Grosso, deep in the heart of the Brazilian jungle, and help to make sure he was eliminated. I don't know what was more astonishing— the information that my friend had located this man, who had been a cruel guard in one of the concentration camps, or the plot he had contrived to kill him.

I knew from our past talks that this gentleman was originally from Poland and had been a survivor of the Holocaust. I knew his entire family had been destroyed, with the exception of one brother, and I knew that he was dedicated to doing whatever he could in any way, shape, or manner to hunt down perpetrators of the Holocaust or anyone associated with Nazi war crimes and hurting them. But until now I didn't know what lengths he would go to.

Still, he was a man I respected and felt comfortable with. I admired him for having arrived in South Africa without any credentials or funds and for making it on his wits and becoming a rich man. So I took his request seriously. Besides, I had never been to Brazil.

But I did have doubts, not so much about the righteousness of his request, but the mechanics of fulfilling it. I knew there would be problems getting into Brazil without receiving an immediate visa, but he said it could be done. There was the issue of travelling with the weapons I had brought with me on safari, but he said that could also be taken care of.

Since the mercenary had already been hired to do the job, my chief task was to bring a substantial amount of cash to Brazil, which would be the reward or pay-off for the death of this Nazi. As an American citizen, I could carry as much U.S. currency as I wanted, but if I were discovered with that large amount of cash by customs agents in Brazil or South Africa, it would make me a suspect because it would be unreasonable for a person dressed in khaki clothes, the way I travelled, to be carrying that amount of cash—unless he was up to no good. But my friend assured me that if I decided to take on the task, I'd get through both South African and Brazilian customs without any problems. Somehow it never occurred to me to ask him if he could guarantee me there'd be no problems with the mercenary I'd have to contact. Nor did my friend offer such a promise.

Putting questions aside, I didn't really think long before giving my answer. I had just come off a safari and that "Boy Scout" feeling or adventurous spirit I always felt in the bush was still with me, so I said I'd do it. I didn't phone Edna to discuss it with her; in fact, I didn't even tell her about it until three months after I returned home. I just told my friend "yes."

After taking care of all the details the next day, he gave me a package of twelve thousand dollars in United States currency. The cash was wrapped in a brown paper bag, and the whole package looked like a loaf of rye bread. My instructions were to meet the mercenary in São Paulo and to stay with him in order to verify that he had eliminated the Nazi perpetrator of crimes against humanity.

When I arrived at Jan Smuts Airport in Johannesburg, I saw how quickly my friend's connections had been able to smooth things out. My name was paged on a loudspeaker, with information to report to a customs agent; my luggage was immediately okayed, and I boarded the plane bound for Rio de Janeiro. I'm not the kind to dwell on negative thoughts, so I have to confess that instead of being apprehensive, I actually had a comfortable flight.

But when we reached Rio de Janeiro, things didn't go smoothly. I was not paged as I had expected to be and instead I was lined up with all the other passengers going through customs. I was busy trying to come up with an explanation for carrying all that cash when it became my turn to have my luggage inspected. The brown paper bag, containing the currency, was in one of my suitcases and the agent was just about to open it up when suddenly two men walked up to him, said something in Portuguese, flashed some badges, and immediately closed my bags and put me in a taxi.

I had a couple of days before my appointment with the mercenary in São Paulo, so I decided to stay in Rio. I had heard so much about the city, its beaches like Copacabana and Ipanema, and the magnificent bodies of tanned men and women you could see there. I roamed the city, visiting some of the squalid *favellas* or slums, and even attending a voodoo ceremony. I was like an excited tourist, and although I had all that money, the thought of what it was actually going to pay for stayed remote in my thoughts.

Finally, it became time to put the plan into effect and I left for São Paulo. I was due to meet the man in a specific hotel lobby between 10:30–11:00 A.M. on any one of three mornings. Since commercial hotels accommodate clients who are met by suppliers between 7:30–10:00 A.M., emptying out the lobbies afterward, it was going to be fairly easy for my appointment and me to spot each other, even though we had no photographs of each other. On the second day of my walking through the lobby, a young man approached me and asked in a European accent, "Are you ready?" That had been our agreed-upon password, so I told him to wait five minutes until I retrieved the money from the hotel safety deposit.

When I returned to the lobby, he told me we were leaving for an airport and that I shouldn't check out of the hotel. I had landed at the main airport in Santos, a ninety-minute drive away from São Paulo, so I was surprised when he directed our cab driver to a small airport ten or twelve minutes away from the hotel where we had met. There was a four-place, single-engine airplane waiting for us, with a pilot who spoke only Portuguese. Our destination, I was told, was a small village a little more than two hours' flying time away.

In the plane, the mercenary told me he was thirty-one years old and that he had been born in Austria, but he had lived in many places in Europe. He was a man who made his livelihood by being a paid killer, which was the reason my South African friend had hired him. But it was all business with him—he had even been hired through an agency.

As we flew over rough terrain, the Austrian and I

reviewed his plan to do away with the Nazi. Each of us had sketches of the man, which we were to destroy before taking any physical action. He ran a trading post in a remote jungle village, and his execution was planned to be carried out during a festive market week when people from the countryside around this outpost came in to sell their meat, vegetables, and any other wares they had.

The trip took us over some of the most rugged and foreboding land I had ever flown over—full of small hills, rocks, and heavy jungle. I was worried about where the plane would land, since the Mato Grosso jungle is the least populated area of Brazil; but an even greater concern came when I saw that the petrol gauge was getting down to zero. I asked how the pilot intended to refuel, but since he couldn't answer me, the Austrian told me that they had deposited enough petrol at the village we were heading for. When he and I left the plane to locate the intended victim, the pilot would take care of the refueling.

As we got ready to land, I looked down, but I couldn't see a damn airport or even a landing field. When I asked, "Where the hell are we going to land?" the pilot gathered what my concern was and pointed to a clearing just below us. After circling around for a few minutes, he brought the plane to a comfortable landing.

In addition to a sketch of the man we were after, the mercenary and I knew some other details about him. He had taken on a different name, married a Brazilian Indian, and had four or five children with her. His trading post was on the outskirts of the village, so we set off for it through the crowds of people. Because of the market, the small jungle settlement of 400–500 people had grown in size to between 3500 to 4500 people, and there was a general carnival spirit, with all kinds of music and games being played. It was hot and muggy, but I really don't remember feeling very much of anything at this point.

When we reached the Nazi's compound, it was a fenced-in area about twenty yards by thirty yards. His wares, which were mostly household goods, bolts of fabric, rubber tires, and various sundry items, were spread out under a canopied canvas in front of the wooden trading post. No more than a medium-size shack, it had an open entrance through which we could see the man we were looking for. We did not go into his compound at the time, though we easily recognized him from where we were standing. Very carefully, we proceeded to destroy the picture and information about him. Everything about his physical appearance matched up, even though he had tanned considerably and wore his clothes and hair like many of the natives.

After observing him from a distance, we wandered back through the village and tried to look inconspicuous. We were both in khaki safari clothes, and since Europeans often came through the jungle as mining or forestry engineers, we didn't really stand out. Besides, the village was teeming with celebrating people; there was so much noise, music, and so many hawkers of all kinds of merchandise that no one really seemed to notice us.

Finally, after wandering around to the various stalls and buying a few things we didn't need, the Austrian said, "Are you ready?" Needless to say, I had been somewhat apprehensive before this point, but now I felt a combination of fear and excitement because I had gotten myself into a task and there was no turning back. It wasn't as if I could send him ahead and go wait for him in the plane.

We walked back to the compound and entered the trading post; I waited near the door frame. I knew that the Austrian had his weapon ready for use; it was a small sidearm. He walked right up to the man who was leaning over the counter facing us and pumped two shots into him. He didn't use a silencer, but since he had put the gun right into the man's chest, right near the heart, all I heard was just two dull sounds.

To my immediate surprise, none of the dozen or so people who were in the post with us acted shocked, except for a heavy-set woman standing next to the trader. Her mouth opened wide, but not a sound came out. I assumed she was his wife. The man slumped down; the Austrian turned and walked toward me. He didn't run, and as he went past me, I gave him the package of money.

As we had planned while in the plane, once the pay-off was made, the Austrian was on his own. He was to make his escape, and I suppose he had his own plans. For my part, I was supposed to return to the plane, and I did. My path was clear the entire way, and although I kept turning around, no one followed me. Just as I had counted on, the Portuguese pilot was ready and we took off.

About three months after I left Brazil, I was told by a friend of the South African man who had asked me to go on this mission that the Nazi had died immediately. I am not aware of where he got this information, nor do I know, to this day, the name of the jungle village where the execution took place.

Looking back now, I see that this whole episode could be viewed as a stupid act, since I was putting myself in the hands of a killer. But I did it because of my association with my South African friend, whose judgment I trusted. Truthfully, though, I have no regrets over what happened. The man was a Nazi criminal with a known record of horrible treatment of the victims in his concentration camp. If I were to go back thirty years in time, I probably would suit up in my "Boy Scout" clothes and take part in that mission all over again.

However, I do want to emphasize this was long before my involvement with the Anti-Defamation League. Now when we go after World War II criminals, we do it in a legal and sophisticated way. It takes longer and sometimes the waiting makes us impatient, but we are very effective.

Chapter Eight
Big Business

In the African bush, reality is what you see, smell, touch, hear, and taste every day. You set your pace by the sun; you eat what you hunt for the pot; and your reach extends to the tip of your hands or the range of your voice. Your contacts are limited to the professional hunter and the native tribesmen who are travelling with you. There is no mail, no telephone satellites in the sky. Once, I remember, a professional hunter radioed us for help for his client, who had been badly mauled by a lion. Their camp was about twenty miles away from us, but the radio signals had be sent to London and then bounced back through Khartoum, which finally relayed them to us. So you really live in an isolated world in the bush.

You also live in a totally focused world, alert to the spoor you're tracking and concentrating on noting and reading the natural signals around you—the bend of the grass, the temperature of animal droppings, the absence or presence of other game nearby or vultures in the sky, and the level of water in drinking holes.

When I was on safari, in short, I was *on safari* and that was my world. Nothing intruded into it. But obviously life went on, both at home and in business, and somehow coming back from safari always left me energized and invigorated so I could concentrate on things with fresh strength. During most of the period between the early 1960s to the early 1980s, I went from hunting big game in Africa to hunting big deals in our industry.

Probably one of my most surprising days in business dates back to 1965. My son, Ken, was out of college, and one morning at breakfast, I casually asked him what he was going to do that day.

"I'm going in to work with you, Dad," he replied just as casually. Ken had worked for our company over summer vacations, and it had been the kind of sweaty, back-bending labor I had done when I first started out working for Lazarus—sweeping floors in our non-air-conditioned warehouses, loading trucks, and packing shipments.

While I must have always wanted my son to come into business with me—what father doesn't, after all?—I honestly don't think I ever pressured him into it. I know we never discussed it in advance. When he was in college, Ken took some business courses, but he was never that serious a student and we used to joke that he majored in fun. (I never complained, since I had been an average student myself and only my athletic ability won me a scholarship.)

Still, I was tremendously pleased that day when Ken said he was coming into business with me. Quite honestly, I suppose I was a chauvinist and old-fashioned enough to believe it was my son's place to come to work with me, not either of my daughters'. My wife didn't work once she became pregnant with our first child, and it was only much later, after the children were grown up, that she opened up a discount outlet at our Brooklyn warehouse. I now believe that either my daughter Joan or Jerilynne would have been an asset to our business also if they had shown the desire to come in with us.

My attitude didn't bother our youngest daughter, Jerilynne, who grew up to become a successful school administrator, and the family is proud of her. I visited her at her office in Yonkers, New York, and was delighted to note the respect and obvious affection the staff had for her.

Her husband, Michael, had served his apprenticeship at the Sydney Company, touching all bases of the business. As he needed to be in his own business, he, along with a partner, purchased a company in the infants' and children's mass merchandise field. We had a very comfortable parting, and whenever we could, we assisted his new company.

Mike is a great family man. It is obvious when you see him, Jerilynne, and their son, David, together.

Recently our first daughter, Joan, told me that she regrets not having had the chance to join the family business. But Joan followed a traditional path, and after going to college for two years, she married a marvelous young man—he was handsome, wealthy, bright, a sportsman, and someone I totally respected and had great rapport with. Shortly after her marriage, she had her first child.

I'm the memento collector in our family, and one of the papers I have is a second-or-third-grade autobiography she wrote: "When I am grown up, I will take over my father's infants' wear business. I will be boss of all the stores in New York. I will be good in the infants' wear business. I will retire and be a movie star, a movie and singing star, and that will be my life." Joan's gone into a few small businesses with some friends and been pretty good at it. Maybe I should have paid more attention to her childhood dream.

Ken and I always had a good relationship; it continued in work and still continues today. We thought the same way, and while I took exception to some of his personal ways of life, in business he was sharp and I respected that. With some sons who go into their father's business, people say, "Thank God, his father was born before him." But you can't say that about Ken. He could have made it on his own because he's a hell of a good salesman, a charming guy, and he was terrific at entertaining the buyers and merchandisers I was less patient with as I became more involved in Africa and later on with the Anti-Defamation League.

Ken also took over most of the importing business we did with the Far East and was very good at that too. In fact, the one major disagreement I remember between us was over clothes. I always came to work well dressed; it was my style and I felt comfortable with it. My clothes were custom-made, I always wore a jacket and tie at my desk, and I even had about twenty-five hats I wore when hats were popular—straw hats, felt hats, derbies, bowlers, fedoras, and the finest fur hats.

Ken, on the other hand, was a child of the 1960s. He'd show up in tie-dye shirts, dungarees, and sandals in the summer. It bothered me for a while, until I learned by observation and by questioning that the buyers didn't mind. Maybe because Ken was my son they disallowed certain things, but the bottom line was that they kept buying, and Ken kept producing, so I learned to look the other way when it came to Ken's way of dressing.

I worked with other relatives in my business also, and for the most part, it worked out well. My brother-in-law, Fred, for instance, was a combination brother and son to me and remained with our company for about thirty-five years. I can't speak for my relatives, but I was relaxed about working with them and made an effort not to talk shop when we got together for family dinners at holiday times.

My brother Jerry, who was closest to me in age, being only five years older than I am, even became my partner for a brief time. I gave him 10 percent of the business in 1949, but he sold it back to me one-and-a-half years later at a considerable gain, since it hadn't cost him anything to begin with! I've always believed he did it at the instigation of his wife, who was probably unhappy that he was working for his kid brother. But there were no bad feelings between Jerry and myself, so he came back to work for me a few years later.

In addition to working with my brother, one brother-in-law, my son, and my Uncle George, who knew production well and helped smooth my feathers when they became too ruffled, I also helped put my third oldest brother into several businesses. From time to time, I've also had other relatives working with me, but the only mistake I've ever made in hiring someone and the only relative I've ever had trouble with was my sister's first husband. I suppose he found it convenient to use our warehouse to stock a business he was running on the side—he just found it even more convenient to stock it with our merchandise! Later, my sister divorced him for other reasons.

If I got along well with family members in business, it was probably because of two things: the sense of family loyalty I had been imbued with from a very early age and the respect for my elders I had also grown up with. When I was first starting out in business, I was in my twenties and most of the businessmen I dealt with were much older than I was. They were always "Mister" to me while I was "Sydney" to them—that's why the company got its name, by the way, rather than a more formal "Sydney Jarkow Company" or something like that.

I learned to listen to these older businessmen and to learn from them even if they set negative role models as one gentleman, a Mr. Mahoney, did. He ran a small buying office, and I'd stop by to chat sometimes. I'd noticed that the major buying offices would cater to out-of-town buyers by paying for good hotel accommodations, transportation, theatre tickets, and things like that. They'd also suggest popular tourist sites to see or favorite restaurants to eat at. Mahoney ran a cut-and-dry little business, and he used to tell me he was there to assist buyers in buying merchandise, not to be a tour guide or an entertainment service.

But I disagreed with him; after all, if an out-of-town buyer was coming to New York, he or she wanted to be entertained after work or at least guided properly to the popular spots. I always did whatever I could to make my customers feel welcome, either with Edna or alone. But there were two policies I always followed: the first was to keep my drinking down to a minimum and to discourage my guests from getting loaded and possibly doing something that might embarrass us the next time we met. I also avoided any uncomfortable involvements with women buyers, and in the beginning of the business years, there were many opportunities. There may have been some mild flirtations—I know I was young, relatively nice-looking, and women generally like me—but I don't think I've ever taken advantage of that fact.

That's not to say, though, that I didn't occasionally take advantage of my buyer's weaknesses if they were relatively harmless. I remember one big sale came about because of a buyer's need to impress his date. A merchandiser with a very major company, he was married but bringing his girlfriend to lunch with me at the Four Seasons, a very posh restaurant.

"When are we going to talk business?" I asked him in advance.

"Over lunch; don't worry," he said. In the restaurant, it was obvious he was trying to show his girlfriend how big a man he was because he ordered the most expensive drinks and food.

I knew my role was to help him act out being the "big shot" and since I knew he had his "open-to-buy" with him—a schedule of what his merchandise needs were—I was prepared to help him. As we sat and talked, he kept telling me he needed ten thousand dozen of this and eight thousand dozen of that. For each item or garment he mentioned, I told him we could handle the order and there was no bargaining at all.

"We can supply it," I said. "The price is such-and-such."

"Okay," he said, "write the order," and I took out my order book and wrote it all down.

Of course, the woman was sitting there with her mouth open because apparently he was everything he told her he was. Because the buyer and his girlfriend were my guests, I paid the lunch check, which was considerable, but he wrote an order of $1.2 million! In all fairness, while I played along with his vanity, I didn't really overcharge him for anything. He got good value for his dollar, and we continued doing business together for years to come.

During Ken's partnership with me, the parent Sydney Company continued to be involved in other children's manufacturing businesses, as we had done in the 1940s, 1950s, and 1960s. One profitable venture that Ken took quickly to the top and then liquidated was Jayel Children's Wear. They were a small contracting company that produced children's snowsuits for us on a cut-and-sew charge. This type of manufacturing procedure was and is common in all apparel-producing companies.

In 1975, I heard that the married couple who owned the contracting company were interested in becoming better involved with us because of their ambition to be identified with the retail community. The Sydney Company, by then, was known for being a small conglomerate of six infants' and toddler's wear companies, which had a successful track record with the mass merchandise chain-store trade. While Jayel's facilities were quite small, we all realized that they could enlarge their operations, provided we supplied the sales outlets, the finances, the administration, and most of the direction. In other words, they'd take care of production facilities and we'd do the rest.

One of the weak links in my knowledge of the children's wear industry was that I never really involved myself with production. But I was always lucky in having or getting the right people around me, and this time was no exception. My Uncle George, my mother's brother, was a crackerjack in production knowledge. Even though he was almost twenty years older than I was, at a time when other men would be thinking of retirement, he was a bundle of energy with an uncanny instinct for identifying and correcting production problems.

We decided to combine the strengths of both companies with my son, Kenneth, as president. He directed sales and took over administration. He ran the company for four years until the Jayel partners decided they wanted to quit. The company was making reasonably good money and we probably could have replaced them, but Ken and I were each developing other interests, so we liquidated that business profitably.

The last business venture Ken and I became involved with and the one that put us over the top financially when we both decided to retire from the children's wear business was the Kent Company, manufacturers of infants' and toddlers' blanket sleepers, other sleepwear, and stretchwear.

In the early 1970s, we represented a southern company called "Stay-On Products," which manufactured infants' sleepwear and crib accessories. In fact, one of the company's owners had invented the fitted crib sheet. The Stay-On Company was bought out by Kleinert, a small company on the stock exchange, but the new owners had to honor our contract to sell the Stay-On products.

As a selling agent, we made a lot of money for them and for us, but as time went on, they thought they could do better on their own, so they tried to redraw the contract lines. It was one of the rare times when I wasn't compatible with someone else and the only time in forty-five years of business that I had to hire an attorney for litigation. But we won, hands down, including court costs.

Two Kleinert men, Marvin Coburn and Michael Gans, who had been part of the original Stay-On team, had wanted to go into business on their own for a long time. They had repeatedly approached me to become a partner with them, since I had the capital and sales outlet while they had the know-how to produce and market. Both these men were probably the best men in the industry when it came to their particular areas of expertise.

Until this point in 1977, I felt bound not to violate my contract with Kleinert by starting a competing business. But our court settlement from Kleinert let me extricate myself from any contractual obligations, and Marvin, Michael, and I went into business and called it Kent Manufacturing. They were responsible for the day-to-day work, while they depended on me for the big sales numbers. Because of the long-term track record of the Sydney Company and because of our connections, we were able to go to a K-Mart, Wal-Mart, Sears, J.C. Penney's, or other mass merchandisers and write big orders, whether it was across a desk or over dinner or on a golf course.

Eventually we became one of the biggest manufacturers of blanket sleepers in the world. Parents who live in cold climates love the sleepers because they don't have to worry about their children kicking off their blankets at night. The one-piece sleep-suits, like old-fashioned long-john underwear, are made of a heavy blanketlike material with either a snap or zipper front, and they're guaranteed to keep children warm no matter how cold the winter night gets.

The company was named Kent because the small manufacturing plant that was originally bought was located in Fort Kent, Maine. Eventually, we ran additional plants for the Kent Company in Greenville, and in Liberty, South Carolina, and in Ballinger, Texas. At a time when other manufacturers were turning to cheap labor in the Orient, the blanket sleepers made by Kent Company—and all the other merchandise we produced—were entirely domestically manufactured.

Toward the end of the 1970s and during the 1980s, Ken was becoming quite an outdoorsman and I was becoming more involved with the Anti-Defamation League and doing quite a lot of travelling for them. Then, around 1985, after about seven years or eight years of running it profitably together, Marvin and Michael approached us with the idea of selling the Kent Company. As production people mainly, they had never had their hands on any real money before. Now, as minority share-holders in Kent Company, this was their first chance to touch it.

Since Ken had become quite an adventurer like I had been, he also decided he didn't want to be in the business any more. In fact, the only difference between my son and myself was that while I had gone after big game in Africa, Ken went white-water rafting in China and New Guinea and other places in Asia. With time, he gradually became more interested in that type of life. But while I always knew I had to come back from Africa, that I had to return to business, I don't think Ken felt that same pull.

I think I must have known for a long time that Ken wasn't long for the business. To him, it was a means to an end. Maybe that was only natural. After all, the business had been my baby, something I had started, but he had just walked into it, so perhaps that's why he didn't have the same deep feeling for it.

Truthfully, I would have preferred that the business continue on to my grandchildren, particularly to Ken's son. But it wasn't my style to force this on Ken, so I let go. I had never used parental power or guilt to control my children, and I wasn't about to start now. I think that I have a dominant personality, but I'm not a domineering person. That's not to say I don't ever find fault with people or I can't be a son-of-a-bitch sometimes; I can be. But I'm also basically very tolerant and understanding, and I've never made demands on my children or on anyone else.

Still, without Ken, and Marvin, and Michael, the excitement of running a business by myself wasn't attractive to me. Maybe I was beginning to find a substitute diversion for my time and attention with the Jarkow Institute for Latin American Affairs, which I helped set up as part of the Anti-Defamation League in 1986. Whatever the reason, I was ready to step away from the business and go on to another phase of my life.

So we called in the business brokers, who went through our books, liked what they saw, and had Gerber Foods contact us with an initial offer that we couldn't turn down. Because we had a healthy business and kept such clean books, something I had always demanded from all of my business partners over the years, the sale was relatively easy and went through in 1985. Gerber was primarily cash-heavy, and we had no objections to taking the cash instead of part cash and part stock, which most other companies were accepting at that time. The purchase price was split five ways between Mike, Marvin, me, Ken, and Marvin's son, Mark, in the percentage of stock that each of us owned.

Up until the last moment, the excitement of stalking prey and the kill instinct were still there for me, even though by this time making money was more of a game for me than a necessity. That's why we tried to get as much from Gerber as we could.

We all walked away from that deal considerably richer than we had been before, and I was already fairly comfortable in a financial sense. But I've always been fortunate because in the forty-five years I was in business, there never was one year when I didn't make a profit. True, the numbers were commensurate with the size of the businesses I bought and ran, but I never had a year where I didn't make money.

Sydney Infants Wear and later the parent business, the Sydney Company, were always privately owned by myself and my family because I never wanted to lose control by going public with the company. It was organized along sub-chapter S lines, which meant that at the end of the year, the stockholders took the profits out of the business, after paying the proper taxes, so the business always ran on a year-to-year basis. My policy was to take the profits and put them into some financial protection—municipal bonds, real estate investments, and so forth.

I've always been a saver, maybe as the result of seeing the hard times my family went through when I was young. I'd put aside a minimum of ten percent of what I earned no matter how little it was—if it was eight dollars a week, I still saved eighty cents. The only time I didn't have any money saved was when I went into business with four hundred dollars. But even when I was paying off my loan to Elias Krupp, I still saved another part of my income and pretended I wasn't earning it.

Initially, I put most of the profits back into the business, since I've always liked doing things on a cash basis. In my private life, I've never carried a mortgage except for my first house and I've always paid up-front for my cars. In business also, I've never liked taking out loans, although, of course, I've sometimes had to. But I never personally guaranteed a loan for business;

if the banks didn't think the companies were strong enough to qualify for the loan, I just didn't take it. I don't know whether I acted that way because of my father's business problems or not, but it was an important business principle for me.

Ken stayed with the Pixie Playmate operation for another year before opting for early retirement. I've kept my financial interests in Pixie Playmate, although I no longer take an active role in it. Through the years it's become a large playwear operation, and the Florida property it's located on, as well as the land surrounding the plant site, has appreciated. Through Pixie I've come to feel closer to Harold Lopatin than to my own brothers. He and his son, Jeff, a wonderful and talented young man, manage the company today.

My years in business have been happy ones; we've gone through ups and downs and had our share of aggravations and problems that business brings, but we have also gained the friendship and affection of the people who have been our partners and associates. We remain good friends today with all of them, which is indicative of the way my former partners feel about me and my family. I've always maintained that if a deal was a good deal, it was good for everyone involved.

In retiring from business in 1985 when I was seventy years old, I thought of it not just as the end of one part of my life but also as the chance to plunge into another part of life. On one of my last African safaris, a hunter taught me that you could climb a hill without getting tired by facing away from the hilltop and walking up backward. I like to think that at this stage of my life, I am still climbing up hills and meeting challenges, even though I might be facing in a different direction than before.

Chapter Nine
The ADL and the Jarkow Institute

As a husband and father, I've long been aware of the importance of an insurance policy to protect my family. That same need for protection applies to business as well, so almost from the start, our companies have been covered by various insurance policies. But it's only been for the past eighteen years that I've been aware of an entirely different kind of insurance—that offered by the Anti-Defamation League. The Anti-Defamation League has never been considered a philanthropy by our family; instead, it's a form of insurance for the honorable survival of the Jewish people all over the world and for the end of discrimination against people of all nations, races, and colors. That's why it's increasingly taken up so much of my life for nearly two decades.

I became involved with the ADL almost by chance, but working with them has tied together many threads of my life—my love of adventure, my experience in dealing with people, and my tendency to help people and fight for fairness.

It all began in 1973 when the children's apparel industry in New York City chose to honor me at an Anti-Defamation League luncheon. The aim in selecting an honoree for this type of affair is to pick someone with recognition within a specific industry or community in order to draw together a lot of people who, hopefully, will pledge funds to your organization or cause.

Up until this point, our family had been active in the March of Dimes. At one time, I was the chairman of the division in Nassau County, a major county in the New York City area. We participated in other non-sectarian charities as well as those connected to local churches. We also took part in some of the charitable and social life of our Long Island synagogue, but it had never filled a major part of our lives; nor had I ever been particularly active in any religious organizations, so I liked the fact that the ADL was not limited just to Jews either in its memberships or in its goals.

When the ADL was founded in Chicago in 1913, its purpose was not only to stop the defamation of Jewish people but to secure justice and fair treatment for all citizens alike. In other words, it fights for broad human rights and appeals to my sense of fair play. That's why over the years the ADL has been just as active in preventing civil rights abuses against blacks or human rights violations against Guatemalan Indians or any other group discriminated against unfairly as well as defending the rights of Jews.

But that's getting ahead of the story. At the time I was going to be honored, I had contributed some small amounts of money to the ADL. But I decided to find out more about the ADL before my name became associated with it at the luncheon. I went over to their headquarters, and a young man named Abe Foxman showed me around. He's since gone on to become the ADL's national director, and it's because of his enthusiasm and knowledge that I've come to regard him as my mentor in the ADL.

As part of the tour of operations, we went into a room full of file cabinets containing historical archives and detailed records. Two men in gray suits and brown shoes, as I recall, identified themselves as agents of a federal bureau. They were looking at files the ADL kept on civil-rights abuses in the South. I asked them why they were looking for information from the ADL files, and one of them cupped his hand to his mouth and said, "The people here have more material by accident on the Ku Klux Klan than we have on purpose in Washington, D.C." I decided then and there if the ADL was valuable to the federal government, then it was good enough for me and I'd be proud to be honored by it.

From about 1973–1983, I served as co-chairman of the Infants and Children's Wear Division. Initially, my role was as a fund-raiser—not so much by directly selling people on the ADL but indirectly by sharing contacts with them and being a role model as someone who was involved and gave generously. But soon I began sitting in on policy meetings.

The ADL is staffed by professionals; for example, Abraham Foxman, the national director, is an attorney; Ken Jacobson, a director of international affairs, is an historian; and Rabbi Morton Rosenthal, whom I'm most involved with on a day-to-day level, is a graduate of the Wharton School of Business. But the organization also relies on input from lay leaders—people in a variety of businesses and professions—and we each have expertise to contribute.

For instance, as a businessman it's necessary to be skillful at dealing with people and in favorably negotiating with them. You need to know how to reach people properly, how to communicate with them, and how to handle everyone from a chief administrator to the head of shipping. Those are the same skills the ADL needs to use when dealing with governments whether we're lobbying for support for Israel, against any discriminatory abuse, or arranging for the extradition of Nazi war criminals. Because of my background in dealing with people, I've been able to contribute advice to ADL leaders who, in turn, like to bounce their ideas off me on occasion.

Additionally, with the support of knowledgeable ADL professionals to brief me, I've done more and more public relations work for them by speaking to different groups and meeting a variety of political and religious leaders, including Pope Pius in Rome and Pope John Paul on his Miami visit in 1987. Through these meetings, groups of us have helped to foster favorable attitudes toward world Jewry by educating legislators, the military, and the clergy.

I've also been able to promote ADL causes on my travels. Two trips I took on behalf of the ADL especially stand out in my mind: one was a good-will journey to Africa and the other was a fact-finding mission to Guatemala.

The African trip occurred in 1982, just two years after my last hunting safari. A group of six American Jewish businessmen, including myself, made our first stop in Nairobi. Our purpose was formally to thank Kenya for helping Israel stage the rescue raid in Entebbe, Uganda, in 1976. Palestinian terrorists had hijacked an Air France flight carrying more than a hundred Jewish and Israeli citizens. Idi Amin, Uganda's dictator, supported the PLO, so his East African air field became a convenient place to land. After a week of futile talks, Israeli commandos staged a well-planned, secret raid, freeing all the hostages. Commando leader Lieutenant Colonel Yoni Netanyahu, brother of Israel's Deputy Minister of State Benjamin Netanyahu, was the only fatality.

Israel is more than two thousand miles away from Entebbe, and Kenya had allowed Israeli airplanes flying this mission to refuel in Nairobi. The raid would not have been possible without the close cooperation of Jomo Kenyatta, president of Kenya at the time. Since regional phone lines for all of East Africa were linked through Nairobi, Kenya had also helped by shutting down all telephone lines in and out of Uganda during the mission.

Jomo Kenyatta had died in 1978, so we met with his successor, President Daniel T. arap Moi. We stayed in Nairobi for only three days, and it was a whole new experience for me because I was travelling in a suit and a tie, not in my "Boy Scout suit" or a bush jacket and shorts. Where once I had gone to Africa to hunt, now I was going as a diplomat. In the past the only business I had to do with officials was to arrange for hunting permits; now we spent most of our time in conferences with government officials and no time at all in the game parks.

Still, in a way I guess I was still hunting for something and that has continued, firm support for Israel. Kenya and Israel enjoyed a reasonably good trade arrangement, and we wanted to encourage its future. I was glad to use what networking connections I had, to name-drop that I had met Jomo Kenyatta years earlier, and to do whatever I could to bolster the image of Israel.

After short stops in Zimbabwe and Zambia where we met with more government representatives, we flew into Kinshasa, the capital of Zaire. Zaire was the first nation belonging to the Organization of African Unity to reestablish diplomatic relations with Israel following the 1973 Yom Kippur War and the ensuing Arab oil embargo. We were accompanied by the new Israeli ambassador to Zaire; our purpose in going to this central African country was to participate in the ceremony installing Israel's new ambassador, and we were given the royal treatment.

Part of this meant touring the various institutions and farms that President Mobutu Sese Seko ran. Mobutu was justifiably proud of one showcase farm that produced something like two million eggs and had over 150,000 piglets on it. We were led to believe he originally had a team of Belgian experts running it, but they didn't work out; then he brought in a Chinese group, but they did no better; and finally a private Israeli team came in and they made the grass grow, so to speak. They increased productivity, helped set up a desalinization plant on the small corner of Zaire that touches the ocean, and did all the proper things, so Mobutu was inclined to favor a relationship with Israel.

Now, Zaire had taken the lead in encouraging other West African countries like the Ivory Coast, Ghana, Benin, Togo, and Nigeria to recognize Israel, and we were on a sort of diplomatic mission, so I had to respect that. But Mobutu himself was pompous and did not appear to be a benevolent leader of his country. A former sergeant in the army, he had staged a coup and helped overthrow and kill former prime minister Patrice Lumumba, I had been told. He had gotten himself elected president and then after a year announced they were going to elect a president for life, with himself as the prime candidate; naturally, he won the election. But politics, as they say, makes for strange bedfellows and it wasn't my place to criticize.

Mobutu himself was tremendously wealthy and loved doing things in the grand manner. He threw one party for us on his private yacht, which seemed to me to be a reconditioned Staten Island ferry. It had its own helicopter pad, and after waiting for him for thirty minutes, we saw his helicopter come floating in. Six tall, black bodyguards got out and he followed. He was a very military-looking man who wore a uniform complete with wide epaulets and four rows of ribbons on his chest. He strode out carrying a riding crop under his arm and wearing a leopard-skin peaked cap on his head. Once the introductions were made in French—the official diplomatic language, since Zaire had been a protectorate of Belgium—the entertainment got under way.

Another time we got to see a different side of this former peasant soldier. It was after an official luncheon, which included representatives of the United States government as well as our group. Mobutu was expecting part of a $20 million aid package from the United States and questioned us about why it hadn't come through yet. We had been briefed by State Department people earlier that he hadn't gotten the increment because Zaire hadn't made a payment on the loan they had already gotten from us the previous year. We had also been told that Mobutu's personal wealth amounted to $4 billion in property and other assets.

At this point, I was acting as the group spokesman—a task we rotated around—and answered that I thought one reason the increment wasn't forthcoming was because of previous unpaid debts. "We know you to be a very benevolent man and it would be an act of great consideration for your people if you could help the government pay its yearly debt," I suggested. With this, he got mad as hell, slapped his riding crop against the table, and stomped out of the room. But a little later, he cooled down and returned. Maybe he even respected me a little for speaking up to him because he requested my presence on later visits he made to New York and Washington.

Despite that one time that I allowed my personal feelings to show through, I was getting more experience in representing the ADL, so in 1983 I was asked to become the co-chairman of its Latin American division. The Latin American Affairs department realized that they faced an array of problems that threatened their security. In working with different political and religious leaders and the Jewish communities in Latin America, the ADL has made its resources and expertise available to build bridges of understanding to the Catholic Church, to fight anti-Semitism, and to counteract anti-Israel propaganda.

I loved Africa but despite some sizable Jewish communities in Nairobi, Salisbury, and Johannesburg, the ADL doesn't play a significant role there. It is, however, vitally important in Latin America. First, the people who live there live in an overwhelmingly Catholic continent. There are more Catholics in Latin America than in any other region of the world, and in the 1960s when the ADL was asked to become active in Latin America the Catholic Church was not particularly friendly to Jews. Pope John Paul may have brought up the Holocaust by referring to "never again" when he spoke to us Jews in south Florida, but the traditional anti-Semitism rooted in Catholic teaching has borne bitter fruit for them in Latin America.

Second, because of anti-Semitism, Jews were regarded as outsiders in their own countries. Even those who were second-or third-generation Argentinian or Chilean, for instance, were never considered Argentinian or Chilean by extreme nationalists.

Third, there were two other threats to those in Latin America. Many Nazis had established strongholds there after World II and because of their wealth and property, usually drawn from illegally confiscating material possessions of Jews who became victims of the Holocaust, they still had political influence. There were also more Arabs living in Latin America than Jews—between two-to-three million Arabs in Brazil, for instance, as compared to 150,000 Jews—and they engaged in anti-Semitic activities and campaigns to encourage Latin-American countries to break relations with Israel.

So despite a strong background in Africa, I took the Latin American assignment I was asked to assume. Since then, I've learned about and travelled to many different Latin American countries—Mexico, Argentina, Guatemala, Panama, Costa Rica, and Brazil—and while Africa is my first love, Latin America is a close tie now.

If Abe Foxman was my original mentor in getting me interested in the ADL, Rabbi Morton Rosenthal is my personal "rabbi" in having involved me in Latin American. He's been director of the Latin American Affairs Division since its beginnings in 1966, and among his many achievements, he helped secure the release of Jacobo Timmerman, the Argentinian newspaper editor, as well as other Argentinians and

Uruguayans imprisoned for political reasons. He mediated relations between the American Jewish community and Mexico following Mexico's United Nations vote condemning Zionism, and in 1983 he briefed President Reagan on anti-Semitism in Nicaragua.

On a personal level, I have the deepest regard and affection for Rabbi Rosenthal and that may be why he also succeeded in persuading me to fly with him in a helicopter over guerrilla-held mountain hideaways in Guatemala.

We went to Guatemala in 1985 at the invitation of a presidential aide. Guatemala did not have a strong background in human rights, and they sought to set the record straight by asking us to assess the situation. It's ironic that they asked ADL representatives to do this because one of the first cases requiring ADL intervention took place in Guatemala in the 1960s. At that time, the Guatemalan vice-president was also editor of a newspaper that began to reprint a portion of the Protocols of the Elders of Zion, an infamous anti-Semitic tract, in each edition. One day he announced in an editorial that he would drive the Jews from Guatemala when he became president.

The twelve hundred Jews in Guatemala felt unequal to the threat, so they turned to the ADL. Through our lobbying in Washington, D.C., protests to the Guatemalan ambassador, and the quiet intervention of the U.S. government, the man backed off.

Now, the potential human rights abuses involved not Jews but native Indians living in the highlands of Guatemala. By 1985, Guatemala had been in a prolonged civil war against guerrillas armed and backed by Cuba, Nicaragua, and Russia. Since the Indians lived in the mountains near rebel camps, they were often caught in the cross-fire between the army and the guerrillas. There had been frequent news reports about massacres of native Indians, and the government's objective in inviting us was to counter this adverse publicity.

The few days we spent helicoptering from village to village and to different refugee camps were most interesting and exciting. Many of the officials we met had to remain anonymous in order to avoid guerrillas intent on killing them.

Our objective was to investigate the living conditions of these Indians. The vast majority of them had had their villages plundered and their crops and possessions taken. Often they were caught in a bind between the rebels and the Guatemalan army; if they gave in to guerrilla demands for food and help, they would be punished by the army. But if they cooperated with government forces, they would face reprisals from the rebels at night.

Often, the Indians were left to fend for themselves and to seek refuge wherever they could. Many tried to make their way north to Mexico. They lived out in the open, growing what they could, killing whatever small animals they could find, and their clothing and living conditions were threadbare. At high mountain altitudes, the temperature was chilly even in the daytime. Children walked around barefoot, wearing just a long shirt while their heads were covered with colorful, knitted woolen hats.

When we found pockets of people, we gave them whatever small supplies of clothing, seeds, and medical supplies we carried with us. The bulk of relief food, clothing, and medicine had been donated by various organizations and was being kept in Costa Rica. Once we assessed what the needs were, we radioed this information on to headquarters, which made arrangements to transport the supplies by overland truck.

Rabbi Rosenthal and I travelled in a French-made Allouette helicopter, which seemed like nothing more than a plastic bubble on some thin, iron girders. A Guatemalan major and lieutenant flew as pilot and co-pilot, and we literally looked down below us, between our legs, trying to spot people.

The problem was that whenever we found them, we never knew in advance whether they were friendly people or hostile guerrillas. On a few occasions, we started to come down to what we thought were refugee camps, only to hear bullet shots on the underbelly of our helicopter, indicating that we were *not* welcome. Part of me kept saying not to worry because I was flying with my "rabbi," but another part of me kept praying that the helicopter would get up as quickly and as high as possible because we had been told that while the rebel's weaponry had power to about forty-five hundred feet, the helicopter had the power of altitude to nine thousand feet.

History and time, unfortunately, proved that the decision to create a Latin American Affairs Department for the ADL was wise and necessary. Between 1966, when the department was started, and 1983 when I became co-chairperson, the situation for Jews worsened.

In Argentina and Uruguay, Hitler's "night and fog" tactic was used and Jews were abducted from their homes and places of work and never seen again. In other countries like Colombia, Jews were kidnapped and asked to pay millions of dollars in ransoms. Nazi literature was widely distributed, and dictatorships denied Jews and others the protection of law. In Argentina, especially, many Jewish and non-Jewish young men and women "disappeared" because of political reasons. I met with some of the "Plaza de Mayo" mothers who protested on a weekly basis to demand the release of the children, and the ADL has been as active on the behalf of the non-Jews as on the behalf of Jewish prisoners.

The weapon the ADL uses is to enlist the help of fair-minded officials, clergy, the law, the U.S. State Department, and the ambassador or embassy staff of the country involved. We compiled a list of twelve hundred Jews who "disappeared" in Argentinian jails from a total of nine thousand "disappeared." We made representations to the Argentinian ambassador and president and to Uruguayan officials. American ambassadors and congressmen on visits to Latin America were asked to intercede on behalf of Jewish and non-Jewish prisoners. In some cases, we did help win freedom for them. But in letting these nations know we were closely monitoring their human rights abuses, we also helped to dampen their government's toleration of anti-Semitic campaigns.

The ADL has also played an important role in trying to bring Nazi criminals hiding in Latin American to justice. The League's way is much more legitimate than the way I once took, and they've completely disavowed any connection with my earlier escapade. "We have to watch out when some of our members might embroider the truth a little bit, but with you we have to worry when you tell the bare facts," Abe Foxman once told me.

So far, only Adolph Eichmann was ever taken out

to stand trial in Israel, but the ADL has helped identify other top Nazis. In recent years, we've pressed for action and Walter Kutschman was arrested and held for extradition from Argentina to Germany. He died in jail, but I believe he may have been poisoned by the Nazi network to prevent a trial and the resultant publicity that would have attracted attention to other Nazis in the region.

But we've located and turned over to authorities the names of seven Nazi war criminals—three in Argentina, two in Chile, and two in Paraguay. Except for one, they're all imprisoned, awaiting extradition to their country of origin, but the proccess is a slow one. Still, because of our persistence, in 1990 Argentina did put Joseph Schwammberger on an airplane to Germany and in 1991 he began standing trail there.

But probably the best proof of the need for the presence of the ADL in Latin America is that our original plan called for us to train one office of professionally staffed human rights workers. Today there are twelve such offfices in Latin America. That's why when Rabbi Rosenthal asked for my support in establishing the ADL's Jarkow Institute for Latin America in 1986, I said yes and pledged a substantial amount to sponsor the Institute. Together, we both thought that an independently funded institute within the ADL could expand existing programs and develop new ones in Latin America. I also felt the need to take a more "hands-on" role.

With the exception of the Guatemalan trip, when I wore my bush clothes again, most of the other work I did for the ADL meant wearing suits and ties. I had missed the chance to go on a fact-finding tour of Argentinian and Uruguayan jails with Rabbi Rosenthal because I needed an emergency carotid artery operation. He and I were on the phone and fax machine two or three times a day, and he described walking through prisons and seeing pictures of Hitler, Goering, and Himmler and hearing German military music playing. He told me about the cruelty and how they had thrown about a thousand young prisoners out of airplanes alive, and my backside burned with the itch to get there, but I couldn't.

I knew that the time had passed for me to do field work and physically track down Nazi criminals.

If I couldn't stalk them in person, if I couldn't jump in actively to right wrongs, maybe I could do something by sponsoring this office. I don't believe that anti-Semitism or injustice has died. I don't believe that because Nazis are old men now, they should be left alone in their last years to die. That's not my philosophy. A criminal is a criminal and still should pay, regardless of his age. I would imagine that they suffered from the fear of being caught, but physical punishment is the best punishment for these bastards. When it comes to Nazis, my philosophy is definitely "don't get mad, get even."

Officially, our object was to make available the ADL method of fighting discrimination wherever and whenever needed in Latin America. "Never leave a lie unanswered," is what Rabbi Rosenthal taught me. We do this by maintaining the largest central archive of information on individuals, organizations, and other factors affecting Jewish life in Latin America.

Once the material is gathered, it's analyzed, interpreted, and disseminated in reports. We also have a computer network linking the Jarkow Institute to human rights offices in major Latin American cities, so there's a constant flow of information to and from ADL headquarters in New York and Washington, D.C.

Additionally, we've expanded ADL programs by providing ADL training for human rights workers in Latin American cities, coordinating activities of these human rights offices, and by working cooperatively with representatives of Jewish and democratic organizations in Latin America.

Currently, we are planning and funding a museum exhibition in 1992 that will spotlight the contributions of Jews in Latin America and commemorate the five hundredth anniversary of Columbus's discovery of the New World. Called "Voyages to Freedom: 500 Years of Jewish Life in Latin America," the exhibit will appear in the United States of America and in major Latin American countries. It's our hope that it will build bridges of understanding between Jews and other groups in America.

In recent years, I've been honored to be elected to important positions in the ADL. In 1987, I became Secretary of the Executive Committee Worldwide, and in 1990 I became a vice-chairman of the National Executive Committee. This was in addition to remaining co-chairman of Latin American Affairs and sponsor of the Jarkow Institute, chairman of the museum project, and vice-chairman of Palm Beach County, Florida, where I live now.

I even became involved in Hollywood, at least in a small way, in an effort to find more funding for the ADL. Several years ago, when I was diversifying my business interests, I invested some money in a movie called *Midnight Express*. It enjoyed some success with young people, and when John Friedman and his partner, Hamilton Fish, asked me to invest in a documentary,

I agreed. It was a documentary made by French moviemaker Marcel Ophuls, about a Nazi war criminal known in France as "the Butcher of Lyons." *Hotel Terminus: The Life and Times of Klaus Barbie* won the 1988 prize for best film at the Cannes Film Festival and went on to win the Academy Award, commonly called the Oscar, in 1989 for best film documentary.

I was proud to be involved with this four-and-a-half-hour documentary, but it wasn't surprising that it didn't enjoy popular, commercial success. Both the length and the subject matter were hard to take. But I felt it would be a valuable asset to the ADL archives, especially when the producers offered it to us with 120 hours of footage about Holocaust victims, Nazis, and accomplices, which were not included in the edited version of the film. Unfortunately, the deal fell through, but it was exciting being involved in a project that won an Oscar!

Although I initially became involved in the ADL through financial contributions, I've done more and more work in diplomatic relations. In the past twenty years, I've gone on many ADL missions to Africa, Israel, and Latin America. As part of the ADL team, I've met with the heads of state of Kenya, Liberia, Togo, Israel, Zimbabwe, Zaire, Mexico, and Panama as well as with the Ambassadors of Nicaragua, Costa Rica, and Israel both in New York and Washington. I've met two Popes in private audiences and participated in meetings with former U.S. Ambassador to the United Nations Jeanne Kirkpatrick, Secretary of Defense Dick Cheney, ex-Secretary of State George Schultz, who deeply impressed me as a straightforward, strong personality, and Vice-President Dan Quayle. When I lived in New York, I was even called on to assist former New York

Mayor Edward Koch in receiving numerous dignitaries, particularly from Africa.

When I list all these things, it makes me wonder really how much I've really given the ADL and how much it's given me. I think the answer is obvious. The ADL has enriched my life in more ways than I can count.

I think back to the lesson my old friend Elias Krupp taught me when I repaid the loan that had helped me buy out my first partner and go into business on my own: that charity is an obligation we have to those less fortunate than we are. I said before, and I meant it, that the ADL isn't a charity but really an insurance policy. But it's also part of my philosophy that we have to give back something of ourselves to the world—whether it's money, time, or involvement.

The ADL has given me more than the chance to travel to exciting places or to meet interesting people. I was doing that before I joined the organization. But the ADL became a satisfying focus for my life at a time when I had almost finished running four or five businesses, raising a family, and going on safaris. More and more, it has taken over the time I had spent on those activities and helped me fill a need to go beyond myself or family interests and find a way to help outside my immediate sphere. Hopefully, the establishment and the endowment of the Jarkow Institute for Latin America will even be able to positively affect the lives of future generations.

You could say that my ADL work is a form of "paying back" something to the world. But as much as I contribute to the ADL, they give me back an equal amount, if not more. I hope that this is one debt that's not settled for many years to come.

The author with the mayor of Jerusalem, Teddy Kollek, May 1992